EN-FD
EPIST/JN
76

F. Mark Walters
4/29/76
$5.31

HARPER'S NEW TESTAMENT COMMENTARIES

GENERAL EDITOR: HENRY CHADWICK, D.D.

# THE JOHANNINE EPISTLES

# A COMMENTARY ON
# THE JOHANNINE EPISTLES

J. L. HOULDEN

PRINCIPAL OF CUDDESDON THEOLOGICAL COLLEGE

HARPER & ROW, PUBLISHERS

NEW YORK, EVANSTON, SAN FRANCISCO, LONDON

THE JOHANNINE EPISTLES. Copyright © 1973 by James Leslie Houlden. All rights reserved. Printed in the United States of America. No part of this book may be used or reproduced in any manner whatsoever without written permission except in the case of brief quotations embodied in critical articles and reviews. For informaton address Harper & Row, Publishers, Inc., 10 East 53rd Street, New York, N. Y. 10022.

FIRST U.S. EDITION

ISBN: 0-06-064020-0

LIBRARY OF CONGRESS CATALOG CARD NUMBER: 74-4634

To Dennis and Ruth Nineham
with affection
and gratitude

# CONTENTS

# PREFACE

The Epistles of John are among the shorter writings of the New Testament. They are not on that account negligible. In the first place, they widen our picture of the Johannine school of thought in the early Church of which the Fourth Gospel is the chief fruit. What is more, they show us something of the life of those Christians who held the faith in the Johannine way. In the second place, they yield a glimpse of a moment in the Church's development which, in certain respects, is always with us. It was a moment, witnessed also in the other later New Testament writings, when the question of toleration within the Church was beginning to arise and the concepts of orthodoxy and heresy started to have meaning. A moment too, at a deeper level, when the claims of speculative theology seemed to conflict with a hold on fundamental Christian verities—about the person of Jesus and about the realities of moral life.

The two matters flow together. It is a question of the criteria for right belief, or, in the words of the title of R. Law's book on the First Epistle, 'the tests of life'.

This commentary aims to bring out these theological questions, as they were raised at that early period of the Church's life. If they remain pertinent, their forms are different; but there are audible echoes, and a study of one period nourishes an understanding of the other.

As is customary in this series, the translation is made by the author. It is utilitarian rather than elegant.

My gratitude is due to Dr Henry Chadwick, Dean of Christ Church, for inviting me to write this book and for making a number of helpful suggestions for its improvement; to Patricia Richardson for making the indexes; and to my companions in the writing of it, John and Celia Cassera, Philip and Susan Sturrock, Chuck Blankenship, and Peter Strange who also kindly read the proofs.

*Cuddesdon,*

ix

# ABBREVIATIONS

| GJ | The Gospel According to John. |
|---|---|
| 1J | The First Epistle of John. |
| 2J | The Second Epistle of John. |
| 3J | The Third Epistle of John. |
| *BJRL* | *Bulletin of John Rylands Library.* |
| Charles | *Apocrypha and Pseudepigrapha of the Old Testament*, Vols. I and II, ed. R. H. Charles, Oxford, 1913. |
| DSS | Dead Sea Scrolls (see Vermes, below). |
| *ECW* | *Early Christian Writings*, translated by Maxwell Staniforth, Harmondsworth, 1968. |
| Hennecke | *New Testament Apocrypha*, Vols. I and II, ed. E. Hennecke/W. Schneemelcher (in English, ed. R. McL. Wilson), London, 1963. |
| *JBL* | *Journal of Biblical Literature.* |
| *JTS* | *Journal of Theological Studies.* |
| LXX | The Septuagint. |
| NEB | New English Bible. |
| *NTS* | *New Testament Studies.* |
| Stevenson | *A New Eusebius*, ed. J. Stevenson, London, 1957. |
| *TDNT* | *Theological Dictionary of the New Testament*, ed. G. Kittel (in English, by G. W. Bromiley). |
| *ThR* | *Theologische Rundschau.* |
| *TU* | *Texte und Untersuchungen.* |
| Vermes | *The Dead Sea Scrolls in English*, ed. and translated by G. Vermes, Harmondsworth, 1962. |
| *ZNW* | *Zeitschrift für die Neutestamentliche Wissenschaft.* |
| *ZThK* | *Zeitschrift für Theologie und Kirche.* |

# INTRODUCTION

## THE JOHANNINE PROBLEM

The three writings with which we are concerned, one of moderate length, the other two very short, do not stand on their own. Together with the Gospel of John and the Revelation they form a Johannine group of writings within the body of early Christian literature, less extensive than but comparable to the Pauline corpus. They are, if we accept that they belong together, the product of a single and distinct group within the early Church. We may, without necessarily accepting the truth of later legends about its origins, label it 'the Johannine church', if we wish to emphasize its institutional aspect, or 'the Johannine school', if we wish to draw attention to its teaching.

The place of the Revelation of John within this group is problematical. It is at best complex, at worst questionable. For our purposes, we shall leave it mainly on one side. But there is no doubt that the Gospel and the three Epistles are closely related, so much so that it is always open to discussion whether they come from one and the same hand (cf. pp. 37 f.).

While it is almost certain that all these writings date from the very end of the first century after Christ or the early decades of the second, few other facts about them are at all clear. Therefore our problem is to place them on the map of the Christian movement of that period, and, more widely, on the map of the contemporary religious scene. There are three major questions. To what circumstances in the Church were they addressed? What is the relationship (of time, authorship and circumstance) between the four works? What are their affiliations in the thought of the time? It is not easy to keep these questions separate. The first two particularly run into each other, and certainly the attempt to answer any of them illuminates the rest.

## THE SITUATION

A good detective, if we are to believe the writers of fiction, does not give his main attention to the blood-stained dagger that lies beside the corpse, but to the minute patch of chipped paint on the window-sill or maybe the infinitesimal stain of mud on the sleeve of the otherwise immaculately turned-out butler. So it may be that we should look for clues to the circumstances of the Johannine Christians (if we may so call them—whether they would have answered to the title we cannot know), not in the long and familiar Gospel, nor even in the relatively substantial First Epistle, but in the slighter works, easily passed over—the Second and Third Epistles; and particularly perhaps in the last, which is full of personal and circumstantial detail and (it is surprising that a Johannine pen was capable of it!) almost wholly devoid of theology.

That does not mean that it invites easy interpretation. We cannot simply read off from this little work all the information we seek. The speck of mud leaves the sleuth still much work to do. But it is a veritable searchlight-beam, from this point of view, compared with the longer works. It is not that they wholly lack information of this kind, but almost all of it is brief, oblique and enigmatic. Little of it compels a single, clear conclusion, as a survey, leading us back to the Third Epistle in due course, and equipping us on the way, will demonstrate.

Consider, for example, GJ xxi. 24. Here is a statement in which the writer addresses us face to face. He looks up from his story of past events and speaks directly out of his own time and situation. But the evaluation of his words is beyond us. It is not even clear that the person who wrote them is the same as the writer of the rest of the Gospel or any part of it. In fact, they read like a note attached by one who stepped in merely to put his seal on what had been written, and we are entitled to wonder how much he knew of the facts to which he gave his authority. And even if it be true that the Beloved Disciple referred to in that passage (xxi. 20) wrote if not the whole of the Gospel then at least ch. xxi, how much further does that knowledge take us in the search for the circumstances from which the writing sprang? We have reached the end of a *cul de sac*; for the identity of the Beloved Disciple remains a mystery, and even if in this passage it looks as if a real and known person is in mind, references to him in the rest of the Gospel may lead us to believe that he is presented as a symbolic figure—though precisely what he stands for (the typical Christian? the orthodox, that is, in this context, Johannine, Christian?) is unclear.

Another passage is more explicit. In 1J ii. 19 ff. we learn something of the situation which prompted the writing of the First Epistle. Some members of the community have gone into schism. Their separation—it seems not to have been an expulsion—is occasioned not simply by factiousness. From ii. 23 and iv. 2 we see plainly (and less clearly from a number of other passages) that there was a matter of doctrine at stake, and we know that despite the separation, controversy continued between the two groups (ii. 26; iii. 7). Yet details are sparse. We know nothing of the course of events which led to the rupture, nor even the exact degree of its seriousness. We cannot be sure how far the doctrinal disagreement was the real reason for the separation: that such disagreement should lead to such a result leads us to ask certain questions about the structure and authority to be found in the congregation. Perhaps the exercise of power had already become formal and inflexible. We cannot tell, either, which party has the majority. The writer's tone is sometimes sufficiently alarmed to make us wonder whether his supporters were not a mere rump. His faith yields a fundamental assurance (cf. iv. 4; v. 4). But are statements such as that found in iii. 13 ('Do not be surprised if the world hates you') simply an expression of his general dualistic theology or a sign that he feels increasingly isolated as a member of a small, threatened group? But however little we can see of the details, this is noteworthy as the first known instance of disagreement among Christians leading to formal separation—the beginning of a long and weary path in Christian history.

The writer's reaction could hardly be described as eirenic. The rivals are no less than antichrists, their doctrine is as good as idolatry (ii. 18; v. 21). We have reached a stage in the development of Church life where, at least in some minds, doctrine is already too fixed to tolerate diversity, and where the institution is too rigid to go to great lengths to keep dissidents within the fellowship. (We may contrast Paul's firm but hopeful policy in a moral case, 1 Cor. v. 1 ff., and the width of opinion found, for example, in the Galatian and Corinthian churches in his day. Not that this was to Paul's liking, but we find no hint of anyone, whether Paul or those from whom he differed, taking their disagreements to the point of separation.) The impression the writer of 1J gives is of tenacious and inflexible insistence on a small number of points which he hammers again and again.

Later we shall feel bound to turn to sober speculation, but while we remain within the limits of the evidence, 1J will take us no further. The Second Epistle, however, yields a few more details about the relationship between the writer and the congregation he addresses. (Nothing compels us to think that it is not the same as that in 1J.) Thus, he is in a position not only to write but to visit (cf. 3J 14). This opens up the question of his role, and 2J 1 (cf. 3J 1) gives a point of definition. He is an elder. What does this signify? He feels pastorally responsible for a community with which he does not normally live. What is the source of that responsibility and what light does the title 'elder' shed upon it?

In 1J ii. 13 f., where admonitions are addressed to various groups in the church, the complement to 'young men' is not, as we might expect, *presbuteroi* (the word in 2J 1), 'older men' or 'elders', but 'fathers': as if (may we surmise?) the more natural word had been preempted, as a quasi-technical title for an officer in the Christian body. 'Fathers' and 'young men' may also bear some degree of technical, institutional reference (cf. pp. 70 f.). If so, then perhaps they are officers of the congregation, while 'elder', in the usage of the Johannine community, signifies one with a wider care, who writes and visits and from the setting of his own congregation exercises supervision over a number of others (2J 13; 3J 14). For even if 1J and 2J are destined for the same congregation, the recipients of 3J may be different; and in any case, the reference there to travelling agents points to this conclusion. As parallels to such supervision of a group of churches, we have the writer of the Pastoral Epistles, who adopts the *persona* of Paul, the writer of Revelation, with his seven churches (ch. ii–iii), and Ignatius, writing en route to Rome (*ECW*, pp. 63 ff.).

Certainly, the title 'the elder' is sufficient in itself both to identify and to recommend the writer. He adds nothing to enhance the authority of his position. So it may be that to speak of him as an 'officer' is misleading. His role may be more personal and charismatic than we have suggested. Instead of being an embryonic provincial metropolitan, with responsibility for the churches in a particular area, perhaps he was a man valued for qualities in relation to which his age was more significant: he was 'the elder' because he was 'the Old Man'!

A prominent feature of 1J is its appeal to continuity with the Gospel's first days and with its roots in the historical Jesus (i. 1 f.;

iii. 11): these things are themselves marks of authenticity of faith. Similarly, 2J opts for conservatism as against the novelty and precocity of the dissidents, v. 9, cf. 1J ii. 7. It may be that the writer did not only support this principle but embodied it. Perhaps when he writes that 'we' have seen and heard and touched (i. 1; cf. iv. 14), he is, if not wholly free from exaggeration based on his sense of solidarity with the tradition of right faith, not too far from the literal truth. Perhaps his own witness carried him back to the Church's early days and perhaps this was the main source of his authority. As in the case of the Elder John of whom Papias and Irenaeus wrote in the second century and whose testimony they valued for its link with eyewitnesses of the Gospel events, the title sprang from venerability at least as much as from anything that could be called formal office (cf. Bornkamm, *TDNT*, VI, pp. 659 ff., 676 ff.). And though the association of these 'Johannine' writings (both Gospel and Epistles) with the name of the Apostle or the Elder John is in no way derived from the text and is only evidenced from late in the second century, that Elder is exactly the kind of man who might have adopted the stance taken by the writer of the three Epistles. (No link with the Apostle is likely to be in mind in 2J or 3J, or 'elder' would not have been used instead of the more distinguished title; though see 1 Peter v. 1.)

There is one other puzzle concerning the use of this title. For one as prominent as our elder appears to be—he has responsibility for a number of congregations—it may seem too modest. At roughly the period with which we are concerned, we already know, from the letters of Ignatius of Antioch, of churches where a monarchical bishop ruled with the support of a council of presbyters (= elders), whom he regarded as his subordinate colleagues. But other evidence shows this title used for the ruling body of a congregation (cf. Acts xi. 30; xvi. 23; xx. 17; xxi. 18; Tit. i. 5; 1 Clem. xliv. 5); and it is by no means out of the question that in the fluid situation of the early Church, in some congregations a single man, bearing the title elder, might stand out as representing the church's pastoral authority over others. The contemporary Jewish usage, where the title was given both generally to leaders and more specifically to the ruling body of the synagogue (cf. Luke vii. 3), discourages any inclination to suppose that the whole Church must have used it in a single sense from the early days.

Whatever precise significance 'elder' bears, the Elder of these two epistles is conscious of being a bastion of tradition—one involved in that establishing of criteria for orthodoxy which was so strong a preoccupation of the Church in the second century, both in the main body and in the sects. We cannot tell whether those opposed in 1J would themselves have claimed to be as closely linked with Christian roots as the writer himself—we never hear their side of the story—but certainly the Valentinian Gnostics, for example, were keen to advance such a claim (cf. Ptolemaeus' *Letter to Flora*, in R. M. Grant, *Gnosticism*, London, 1961, p. 190), as were indeed all those many heretics who adopted the name and so the mantle of one of the apostles for their writings (see the contents of Hennecke, *NT Apocrypha*, ed. R. McL. Wilson).

It is worth asking whether the admittedly meagre information to be gleaned from 2J now illuminates features of the longer works which might otherwise seem to have no bearing on our present enquiry. We have already seen that the use of the title 'the Elder' rather than a personal name in the opening address of 2J and 3J accords well with that reliance on continuity from the Church's roots which is so pressing a concern of the First Epistle: such a man is a reliable rock in a sea of competing currents of doctrine. Can we go further and find that light is shed also upon the Gospel?

The teaching about the promised Paraclete, the Spirit of Truth, in the Supper Discourses (GJ xiii–xvii), is often taken as an endorsement of the principle, dear to many in the 19th and 20th centuries, of the Spirit-guided development of Christian doctrine through the course of the Church's history. In particular, there is the statement that the Spirit will lead the disciples into all truth (GJ xvi. 13). But this reading of the evidence, which sees a window giving on to a boundless future, is not the only one, nor is it the most likely to accord with the writer's intention. The Paraclete, the brooding presence guarding the Church for ever, is a conservative not a forward-looking force. His task is to anchor the Church in the things of Jesus: xiv. 26; xv. 26; xvi. 14 f. And, when we come to envisage what the guiding of the Paraclete meant in practical terms for the Johannine church, there is much to be said for the view that the mouthpiece of the Paraclete was the leaders of the community (just as Ignatius, for example, was conscious of being the channel of the Spirit's utterance, Philad. vii, *ECW*, p. 113)—men like the Elder, whose task was to maintain the Church in the authentic paths (see G. Johnston, *The Spirit-*

*Paraclete in the Gospel of John*, Cambridge, 1970, pp. 119 ff.). Insistence upon this principle of conservatism is nothing like as strong in GJ as in 1J, but it is there in germ. And if we need a link between the concept of the Spirit and the leaders who were the Spirit's mouthpiece, then we have it in the reference to prophets in 1J iv. 1-6, only the Spirit of truth is now identified by a different and simpler criterion than anything to be found in GJ—whether his spokesman acknowledges that Jesus the Messiah came 'in the flesh'. To fail that test is to fail utterly.

If the hints in the other Johannine writings prompt certain lines of thought about the situation which gave rise to them, the Third Epistle remains, from this point of view, a gold-mine. Here and here alone in the three epistles are names; here are parties and events, and people moving from one place to another; here are concrete words like 'congregation' (*ekklēsia*), and emotions openly expressed. It is a relief from the abstractions of the rest of the Johannine works.

However, when it comes to saying what the various items of information really betoken, the matter is less straightforward. First, what are the facts? The Elder writes to one of like mind with himself, Gaius, who to judge from *vv.* 3 f. has been under pressure from others whose doctrine differs from his. Gaius is, it appears, a leader of his party; he receives visitors and is the Elder's link with the congregation to which he belongs.

The issue in Gaius' church is not only doctrinal (*v.* 3), it is also political. In 3J the doctrinal issue is in fact never made clear, but the political question is obvious enough. In one aspect, Gaius stands for a non-parochial view. He maintains bonds of fellowship with other congregations, in particular that of the Elder, who exercises an undefined pastoral oversight which extends to Gaius' church (*vv.* 5-8).

Diotrephes, on the other hand, is keen to be free of this link, standing, it appears, for congregational independence—at least as far as the Elder's influence is concerned. He is willing to go to considerable lengths to eliminate this influence from the church (*vv.* 9 f.).

There are two points at which we may use the other epistles to fill out this picture. Gaius and his friends (presumably by contrast with Diotrephes) can be described as living 'in the truth' (*v.* 4; cf. 2J 4). A comparison with 1J and 2J leaves us in no doubt what that is likely to mean. It means accepting that Jesus the Messiah came in the flesh: 2J 7; 1J ii. 21 f.; iv. 2. The dispute between the two groups has reached the point of schism. So it had already in 1J ii. 19, only now the situation is reversed. There, those who refuse to accept what the writer holds to be 'the truth' have 'gone out'; here, they have themselves expelled others, whether fellow-members of his own church or the visitors referred to in *vv.* 5–7. In the one case, it looks as if the 'orthodox' are still in the saddle, in the other as if they are subject to the attacks of a heretical majority. There is much to be said for the view that 1J and 3J refer to different churches. It is not impossible, however, that a single situation was so fluid that it could be described in two ways, and that while from a safe distance it could be regarded in the former, more optimistic way, it looked on closer acquaintance distinctly less promising. We have already noted that 1J has the air of bravely playing down a state of affairs which is more vexatious than is openly allowed. It may be that from the start the Elder faced a congregation which had already largely slipped from his grasp—in both doctrinal and personal loyalty.

From an institutional angle, Diotrephes, it seems, represents a stage in church development otherwise scarcely visible in the New Testament: a point where a congregation wishes to emancipate itself from dependence on those individuals and groups to whom, perhaps, it owed its foundation and both its possession and its formulation of the Christian faith. We have other evidence of congregations living in such dependence—from the early days we see it in the Pauline letters, from a period close to that which now concerns us we see it in the Pastoral Epistles, and both the Revelation of John (ch. ii–iii) and, less clearly, the Ignatian letters probably represent some such situation. But here the monarchical bishop, the single leader of a congregation, begins to come into his own, and a congregation, or some part of it, seeks to run its own affairs, free from the tutelage of venerable authorities (cf. A. von Harnack, *TU*, xv, 3, 1897). There are signs that this was not the only case where this emergence of independent status was not smooth and unchallenged but resulted from positive assertion and defiance (cf. W. Bauer, *Orthodoxy and Heresy in Earliest Christianity*, London, 1972, pp. 61 f., on Ignatius).

But it is not simply a matter of the development of ecclesiastical organization. There is a doctrinal issue, and so prominent is this in 1J and 2J that we must suppose that it was of greater importance than any personal animosities or power struggles.

It is the link between 3J and the other two epistles in relation to the watchword 'the truth' (cf. above) which both confirms the view we have taken of the situation reflected here and rules out the hypothesis put forward by Käsemann, reversing the common reading of the evidence. He held ('Ketzer und Zeuge', *ZThK*, 1951, pp. 292 ff.) that far from Diotrephes being a heretic to whose downfall the respectably orthodox writer of the epistles is devoted, he is, though admittedly greedy for power, in doctrine a traditional and conservative figure; while the Elder is a disaffected and now expelled member of his own church (an elder under himself as 'bishop'), who stands for that speculative presentation of Christianity, Gnostic[1] in tendency and charismatic in expression, of which the Fourth Gospel, in Käsemann's view of it, is the prime literary embodiment (cf. his *Testament of Jesus*, London, 1968). The Elder, together with his allies, such as Gaius, who remains in the congregation, is the enterprising heretic, Diotrephes is the pillar of conservative orthodoxy.

The corollary of this view must surely be that 1J and 2J are addressed to a quite different destination. They attack a more pronounced Gnosticism than that represented by the Elder, so that he himself stands at a middle position within the theological spectrum of his day. One of Käsemann's chief arguments in favour of his thesis is that in 3J the Elder refrains from any exposition of his doctrinal position and from any attempt to refute that of Diotrephes. This is because he is only too well aware of the latter's doctrinal respectability and of his own idiosyncratic and dubious position. He may even hope to be received back into fellowship. Meanwhile he can best angle for support if he confines himself to

[1] The term Gnosticism is used in two related but distinct senses. Traditionally, it has denoted the teachings of a group of second-century deviationist Christian sects which were the object of attack by the orthodox fathers at the end of that period, Irenaeus, Hippolytus and Tertullian. More recently, largely popularized by the usage of R. Bultmann, it has come to signify a more diffuse and general theological culture, bearing the characteristics found in the sects, but discernible already in the first century. We use it here in this wider sense. It is marked by dualism, depreciation of material reality, a fondness for the esoteric and the speculative in religion, and a strong concern for the salvation of a spiritual élite; and was composed of ingredients drawn from Greek, Jewish and oriental sources. See R. McL. Wilson, *Gnosis and the New Testament*, Oxford, 1968; R. M. Grant, *Gnosticism and Early Christianity*, Oxford, 1959; H. Jonas, *The Gnostic Religion*, Boston, 1958.

personal attacks on the leader himself (*v.* 10). If he were, as in the usual interpretation, the authoritative Johannine spokesman, surely he would have explained his doctrinal position in full. Further, in writing to the 'more Gnostic' group, the Elder can recommend that the offenders be expelled from the community (2J 10). Not so in 3J: clearly, because he is powerless to do so. So, in relation to Diotrephes' church, he is a subordinate figure, not asserting authority, but struggling to retain a foothold.

There may be many other reasons for the writer's having confined himself to personal and circumstantial matters in 3J, among them perhaps the decision to limit the length of his letter, as in 2J, to one side of a sheet of papyrus (which it exactly fits). More important, like 2J, 1J as it stands hardly presents its author as an opponent of traditional doctrines: in comparison with the Fourth Gospel, it is a reaction in the direction of 'main-stream' Christianity, with its more conventional eschatology and its stress on Jesus' messiahship (cf. pp. 79 f.). And we have seen reason to suppose that even in GJ, the tendency towards daring doctrinal innovation, free from the shackles of tradition, is hardly prominent (p. 6). And 1J, with its insistence on continuity with 'the beginning', positively opposes any such trend (cf. pp. 48 f.). The living witness, which Käsemann sees as a factor opposing the traditionalism of someone like Diotrephes, is for the writer of 1J a witness to the past, at least in intention—we cannot tell how far he was in a position to carry it into effect.

But whatever the objections to Käsemann's reading of the situation,[1] it has the great usefulness of pointing as sharply as possible to a question raised by all these writings: their place in the emergence of positions that can be labelled 'orthodox' and 'heretical', and of a consciousness of these categories in the Christian body. They pose the question: precisely what made 'orthodoxy' orthodox and 'heresy' heretical? And by what process did particular writings come to be allocated to one category or the other, often being moved—without apology or notice—from one to the other? It is in the setting of these questions that it may be most appropriate to hazard a reconstruction of the circumstances reflected in the Johannine writings.

[1] Bultmann, Commentary, p. 95 n., calls his reversal of the usual reading of the situation, with the writer as an expelled elder of Diotrephes' congregation, a 'fanciful hypothesis'.

One matter of doubt, as we have seen, is whether the three epistles are all addressed to the same church. The greater serenity and generality of 2J speaks for its destination being different from that of the much more fevered 3J. Yet there are clear links between all three writings. Both 1J and 2J speak of persons described as antichrists (1J ii. 18; 2J 7), and 3J shows us Diotrephes, a man who is the object of such strong disapproval that he qualifies well for the title: like the antichrists of 1J he is in schism from the writer's supporters (1J ii. 19; 3J 10). In other words, if two or even three congregations are being addressed, then we must suppose that these Johannine churches are all being exposed to comparable threats—in all the Elder's 'truth' is at stake—whether at roughly the same time or over a period.

If all are addressed to one congregation, then we have to describe the development of views and relationships which they reflect. What story is it possible to tell?

One of our most useful pieces of evidence is the dubious reputation in the second century—from the point of view of the conservatively 'orthodox'—of the Fourth Gospel. It was favoured first, as far as can be seen, by the Valentinian Gnostics, one of their number, Heracleon, writing a commentary on it, and it was uniformly neglected until near the end of the century by the pillars of main-stream Christianity, even by some who might have been expected to be glad to use it in their writings—in particular, Papias, Polycarp and Justin (cf. Bauer, op. cit., pp. 205–12). Only with Irenaeus and the Muratorian Canon (Stevenson, pp. 144 ff.) does this Gospel come into any wide acceptance in indubitably orthodox circles, and even then as the last of the four. One might have expected that its ascription (by them) to one of the leading apostles of Jesus and its high doctrinal content would have earned it pride of place. But it was not so. As far as the central and dominant Church tradition went, it came late on the scene. Its recognition was a new development, the effect probably both of its association by this time with the name of John and the fact that orthodox theology was coming more and more to be formulated in terms (*logos* above all) which found Johannine texts of the greatest service and congeniality.

The Fourth Gospel was in its origins suspect from the standpoint of 'ordinary' Christianity. Wherein lay its fault? No doubt, partly, it was simply too elaborate, too highly wrought in its doctrinal expression. It was much richer in intellectual content than any other early Christian writing we know (except Paul's Romans). But it was also dangerously speculative and abstract, and equally dangerously lacking in emphasis on the historical roots of Jesus; it said nothing, for example, about the circumstances of his birth. It was all too easily favoured (though not quite all of it can have been to their taste, vi. 39 f.; vi. 52-8; xx. 27) by Christians who saw Jesus as a purely spiritual emissary from God to a world sunk in evil, who regarded the material world as effectively outside God's power and concern, and who set so much store by the saving efficacy of the visit of Jesus the heavenly redeemer that they had virtually abandoned any belief in his future return or in such 'earthy' doctrines as the physical resurrection of the faithful which accompanied it. Such a view of GJ is possible: with ch. xvii as his starting-point (it is appropriately chosen), Käsemann, in *The Testament of Jesus*, regards it as clearly tending in this Gnostic direction and frequently, if unreflectedly, docetist in tendency. (See also his study of the Prologue to the Gospel, in *New Testament Questions of To-day*, London, 1969, pp. 138 ff.)

Now there are many passages in GJ which give the lie to such a view. There is a series of references to the Last Day and the coming resurrection of the believers (and in one case unbelievers too), in conventional style (v. 27-9; vi. 39, 40, 44; xii. 48). There are enigmatic references—but clear to the reader 'in the know'— to Jesus' human origins (i. 45; vii. 42-4; possibly viii. 41). There are passages which go out of their way to emphasize the physical reality of his death (xix. 34 f.) and of his risen body (xx. 27; probably xxi. 13), as also of his eucharistic flesh (vi. 52-8). But though these passages can be held to form part of one writer's single, balanced outlook, complementing other statements, many of them look as if they might be corrections to a previously more homogeneous and smoothly running narrative. This is particularly true of the eschatological statements, of the reference to the effusion of water and blood at Christ's death (xix. 34), and of the passage on the eating of his flesh in ch. vi. They are therefore signs of development within the Johannine church: of development in what we may call an orthodox direction, or in the direction of what must have been increasingly felt to be normative Christianity. They are all anti-Gnostic in tendency and all draw the Gospel towards beliefs that are found generally in the writings of the main-stream. These doctrines were all to be touchstones by which the orthodox came to differentiate themselves from the Gnostics.

What is more, they are among the points upon which 1J lays stress, points which receive much greater prominence there than in GJ. Thus, the coming return of Christ and the day of Judgement are, in 1J, no mere addenda, at best one element alongside others with which they can only with difficulty be reconciled. They are at the centre of the writer's mind and a prime reason for the urgency of his attack on the heretics. Indeed, their very existence is itself a sign that the End is near (ii. 18 ff.; ii. 28–iii. 2). It is true that a sense of the Christians' present enjoyment of the redeemed life is equally (if not more) prominent, but this never jars with the assurance of the imminent consummation to quite the extent that it does in GJ. Moreover, this emphasis on the coming acts of God is so strong that 1J returns, in effect, to a more primitive eschatological awareness than that of not only GJ but also other writings of its period (e.g. Luke–Acts and the Pastoral Epistles), for the End is not just a necessary part of a total theological scheme, rounding it off as if for the sake of completeness, or an assured but relatively distant happening: it is on the very threshold (ii. 18). The emergence of false teaching as a desperate threat has, so it appears, awakened this conviction to new life. But the writer of 1J is, by comparison with GJ, a man who finds it not uncongenial, in relation to the rest of his pattern of faith.

Similarly, the genuineness of the humanity of the Son of God is one of his cardinal claims, iv. 2 (cf. 2J 7). And in ii. 22 he asserts that it is Jesus—the human Jesus—and none other who is the saving Messiah (cf. iv. 14). But while this assertion is firmly made, there is a curious feature about it which yields important information concerning the writer. Nowhere is he able to formulate any clear reason for the crucial importance of this belief. It is reminiscent of the constant urging of the necessity for right belief which we find in the Pastoral Epistles, and which is combined with an almost total lack of information about its contents! In the case of 1J, it is not easy to see that his central and reiterated doctrines (viz. that God's chosen offspring abide in the truth and must live the life of love which the truth demands) depend necessarily upon the belief that Jesus the Messiah came 'in the flesh'. This is for him the vital heart of orthodox belief, linking him with the tradition with which he desires at all costs to be associated—but what the connection is remains beyond his powers of formulation. There is much to be said for the contention that many of his doctrinal statements—above all his negative attitude to the world, ii. 15 f.; v. 19—fit only imperfectly with this central dogma. Dogma is the word: it is stated (e.g. in iv. 2) with the flat assurance of a conciliar deliverance. It is as if there were pressures of a type more ecclesiastical than doctrinal which led our writer towards his imperfectly logical statement of faith.

This feature accords well with the general christology of 1J, which is much less 'advanced' and more traditional and simple than that of GJ. The Epistle is a distinctly theocentric rather than christocentric work. Jesus is God's agent, the Messiah, who carries out certain tasks, rather than the mediator who in his very being is one with God (GJ x. 30). While 'God is light' (1J i. 5) and 'love' (iv. 8), there are no statements concerning Jesus comparable to the great 'I am' sayings of the Gospel. Even those passages which seem to speak in 'high' terms of Jesus (i. 1 f. and v. 20 f.) do so only ambiguously and obscurely, especially when put alongside comparable passages in GJ. They give the impression of evading the clear statement of 'high' christological belief.

In 1J then we meet a stage in Johannine teaching which is also encountered in certain, possibly added, passages in GJ. They represent a restatement of Johannine doctrine which lacks both the speculative quality and the power of mind which is manifested in the greater part of GJ. It is a stage which attempts to draw back, under conservative pressure, exerted perhaps from a weight of 'normative' Christianity elsewhere, from Gnostic-type tendencies and towards the teaching of the main body of the Church.

Not surprisingly, some Johannine Christians, even perhaps the majority, were unwilling to accept this development and wished instead to move in the opposite direction. These were the heretics of 1J and 2J. By the time 1J was written they had gone so far as to separate in the name of what they held to be the truth but what the Elder regards as unwholesome novelty (2J 9). If these people are also in view in 3J, then they have by now gained the upper hand in this congregation and are able to expel others—the boot is on the other foot (cf. 1J ii. 19; 2J 11). In the person of Diotrephes they have found a leader capable of standing up to the persuasion of the older, main body.

From their point of view, the position taken by the Johannine 'authorities' was open to serious objections. In the first place, it had come to place far too much reliance on mere tradition—on alleged continuity with the early days. Note the frequent use of *archē*, 'beginning', in this sense (1J i. 1; ii. 7, 24; iii. 11; 2J 5 f.; see H. Conzelmann, 'Was von Anfang war', in Beiheft 21 to *ZNW*, 1957, pp. 194 ff.), alongside its occasional use to refer to eternal origins (e.g. 1J ii. 13), which is by contrast the dominant sense in GJ (e.g. i. 1). It is possible that both sides were glad to play this card; but more probably the appeal to the past, in this simple form, was opposed on the grounds of that conviction of possession of the Spirit which was prized so highly not only by Johannine communities but by other parts of the Church (cf. its prominence, earlier, in the writings of Paul). We have seen that in GJ this had already become a principle of conservatism (p. 6), and in 1J iv. 1-6 the caution goes further. Was this not a reaction against those for whom possession of the Spirit was a certificate for the validity of all new ideas, whereby the Christian present was canonized at the expense of the Christian past?

In the second place, the elements of incoherence in the presentation of the orthodox case which we have noticed must have seemed to the 'heretics' like failures to carry teachings which they all had in common to their proper conclusion. They, the heretics, were consistent where the orthodox were muddled. The dispute was between people whose beliefs were in many ways not far apart— and all the fiercer for that. Thus, we can be sure that the heretics would have shared to the full that pessimistic estimate of the world which is expressed in 1J ii. 15 f. and v. 19. But it was precisely their firm hold on this principle which made it impossible for them to accept that the divine redeemer could have taken genuine human form—'come in the flesh' (iv. 2). How could such a one involve himself with that material reality from which it was his mission to deliver imprisoned mortals?

It is customary to distinguish in discussions of the theology of this period between ontological and ethical dualism; between the belief that the universe consists of two opposing realities, good and evil, between which the whole is divided to its very roots, and the belief that within a single universe, created by God, moral rebellion has taken place and resulted in a warfare, between good and evil forces, whose outcome in God's favour is never in doubt.

It is also customary to hold that while Gnosticism held the former position—it was indeed one of its fundamental tenets—the Johannine writers, in common with Judaism and other Christians, held the latter. In GJ, it is true, the creative work of God, through the Word, is clearly stated (i. 1 f.). But in 1J, while it may indeed be that this is the writer's conviction, nowhere does he put it before us. Here too there is a failure to perceive and state the fundamental issues at stake, which points to a certain mediocrity of mind and no doubt laid the writer open to easy attack.

Again, in relation to eschatology. Both groups no doubt agreed to speak of the believers' present status in terms of the possession of 'life' or 'eternal life' (1J i. 2; iii. 14; v. 11 ff., 20). The gifts associated with the Last Day and the coming new age were already enjoyed by those who had received the anointing and in whom the divine seed had been planted (1J ii. 20; iii. 9). The resurrection had already broken into the present world and established itself in the redeemed community. For those thus assured of the fulness of the present gift, it was hard to see what part any future divine act could play. Was the talk of it not a barbarous Jewish tale, transcended in the sublime doctrine which had been received? How was it possible to look forward to the return of Christ and expect the day of Judgement (ii. 18, 28; iv. 17), when life, the gift of the resurrection, was (as in the belief of others reckoned as false teachers, 2 Tim. ii. 18) 'past already'? It appeared to be a denial of the core of faith.[1]

And was not immunity from sin a fruit of salvation? How then could the orthodox still concern themselves with their troubled consciences and with the quest for forgiveness (i. 8 ff.; v. 16 f.), especially when they seemed to accept the essence of the heretics' position in the matter (iii. 9; v. 18)? They could surely be expected to state their beliefs more clearly. It was of course easy for the orthodox to accuse the heretics of unreality—Christians sinned after baptism, and moral realities could not be evaded. But the heretics had a case which failed to receive a convincing answer in the terms which the orthodox chose to use.

[1] In *The Testament of Jesus*, p. 16, Käsemann epitomized the teaching of the Fourth Gospel thus: 'For John, eschatology is no longer the force that determines christology; the opposite is the case. Christology determines eschatology and eschatology becomes an aspect of christology. In Christ, the end of the world has not merely come near, but is present and remains present continually.' In 1J this position is in part reversed.

# INTRODUCTION: THE SITUATION

The heretics may well have felt that the Johannine tradition, as represented above all by GJ, pointed in the direction which they had taken. Others had committed the error of trying to join to that tradition certain elements, derived from the teaching of intellectually less aspiring Christians. They had acted out of alarm at developments they observed, but their alarm was the measure of their failure to seize the logic of their own original teaching. And the tradition was such that it resisted the assimilation of their importations and they survived only at the expense of consistency and clarity.

Part of the trouble with the orthodox (represented by the Elder) was their reluctance to adapt their methods to changing needs. The term 'elder' in 2J and 3J is the only overt reference in these writings to anyone resembling an officer of the Church (except conceivably the false prophets of 1J iv. 1), and as we have seen the title may well not bear that sense (pp. 4 ff.). These works show no interest in hierarchy, order or organization in the Church. It is conceivable that the picture of the disciples, especially of the Beloved Disciple, in the Gospel bears some relationship to the leaders of the community at the period of writing, but only the giving of authority to forgive or refrain from forgiving in GJ xx. 23 comes near to portraying them as Church officials. And the Beloved Disciple is more likely to represent the true believer or the representative of authentic Johannine teaching than directing authorities within the congregations. And as far as 1J is concerned, it is noteworthy that in ii. 27, the anointing of teaching is apparently given to all members of the community. At least in the negative sense that they say so little about leaders, the Johannine writings present a picture of egalitarianism in the Christian community.

Similarly, the writer of 1J never once appeals to any authority that he possesses by virtue of his position. (Contrast the Pastoral Epistles and the Ignatian letters.) Unless an opening address has been lost in transmission, there is no statement of title or name, no appeal (and this is true also of 2J and 3J) to the power of an apostolic name, such as the writers of the Pastoral Epistles and (unless it is authentically Pauline) Ephesians adopted. He is content to appeal chiefly to the truth of the doctrine which he professes —to its truth and to its age. Alas, the day for the sufficiency of such ways was over. It was becoming increasingly necessary to assert the authority of properly accredited office in the Church.

The need was for men who by their very position could at least claim a right to discipline those whose teaching deviated from the approved lines. Soon not only the true teaching but the position of the officers themselves was to be seen as reaching back to the Church's origins (cf. the succession lists of bishops which begin to appear in the mid-second century, see Stevenson, pp. 12, 73, 117 ff.).

The Elder was responsible for a number of congregations. 2J 5 f. implies that there is a circuit of congregations to be visited. And so many details are given in 3J (especially *v.* 10) which would surely be well known to the immediate recipients that the letter must be intended to be circulated. The groups are linked by letters and, as in Paul's day, by visits from accredited representatives. Paul would have called them apostles, but that is not a Johannine word and we learn of no substitute (cf. Didache xi–xiii, *ECW*, pp. 232 ff.).

In circumstances such as these the Johannine Epistles may have had their origin. They are all part of a campaign to put a brake upon those who would 'gnosticize' the Johannine tradition of Christian teaching. The dilemma of the orthodox is this: they regard themselves as teaching nothing but the Gospel as it had always been, and, whether or not they had knowledge to back up their claim to go back to the beginning, this claim has come to be of vital importance to them. At the same time, their tradition had long, perhaps from the establishment of their church, looked in the Gnostic direction and contained many of the ingredients for the development which was now, to their horror, taking place. The Epistles show those who felt themselves to be the guardians of the Johannine tradition, at a time somewhat later than the emergence of its finest literary fruit, the Gospel of John, engaging in a policy of withdrawal in the direction of simple and main-stream Christian teaching, like that represented by the Gospels of Matthew and Luke. That teaching was characterized by a firm hold on Jesus' genuine human life and death and a belief in his future return. It was strongly ethical, traditionally eschatological. Only in one major point is the writer of the Epistles out of tune with it—in his neglect of all appeal to the Old Testament scriptures (apart from the passing reference in iii. 12). It is possible to see this as another example of his imperfect assimilation of 'orthodoxy'. But the Johannine tradition was far from neglectful of the

Old Testament (cf. the frequently ingenious and skilled use of texts in GJ), and the absence of references in the Epistles may more suitably be ascribed to their inappropriateness in this setting.

To judge from the capture of GJ by the Gnostics in the second century—and indeed from the tone of the Epistles themselves—the opposition was too powerful and the campaign was unsuccessful. For the time being, the Johannine mantle may well have been worn by the heretics. Only the emergence at the end of the century (above all in the Alexandria of Clement and Origen) of a Christianity which needed the Johannine texts because they accorded more than other New Testament writings with its own terminology drew these writings within the orbit of orthodoxy. This Christianity was formally orthodox rather than Gnostic on the crucial issues (belief in God as creator, in his historical purpose, and in Christ's 'fleshlyness'), though it was in many ways highly Gnostic in atmosphere. For them GJ was providential.

But this lay in the future. The Epistles may be read as the testimony to a rearguard action. It failed partly because of the attractiveness at that period of the Gnostic style of thought and life, but partly, it must be confessed, because their writer or writers—the Johannine guardians—were insufficient for the task that confronted them. Understandably, their work fell between two stools: there was no wholesale renunciation of Johannine ideas in favour of 'plain' Christianity; nor was there an attempt to restate the theology of GJ in its pure form—and there to draw a halt. Instead, we find a mixture of both policies—and even some statements (on the world and on the sinlessness of believers, ii. 15 f.; v. 19; iii. 9; v. 18), which go further than GJ towards the position presumably favoured by the opponents. It would not be surprising if this attempt, perhaps partly political, to have the best of all worlds, resulting in the adopting of a number of incompatible positions, failed to carry conviction; however laudable may have been the determination to hold together, if possible, the Johannine community of Christians which knew the teaching of GJ xvii about unity as the legacy of its Saviour.

Above all, the writer of 1J, less penetrating and vigorous in mind than that of GJ, and much more limited in the range of his thought, failed to exploit in his favour the rich christological teaching of the Gospel. As we have seen (p. 14), he preferred to use in relation to Christ a number of relatively simple, traditional categories, but for the rest to be largely theocentric in approach. His failure both to be precise (i. 1) and to be creative in this area may well have been, from the theological point of view, crucial. The signs are that the heretics, refusing as they did to identify the Messiah with a 'fleshly' Jesus, who offered himself in sacrifice on the Cross and would soon return, were by no means lacking in a christology. It is likely that it was of the 'highest' type—that is, that for them the Messiah was a spiritual, angelic figure, sent by God to rescue his chosen ones from the doomed world of matter and flesh: the emissary of light to a universe hopelessly lost in darkness.

In another sense, however, the stand taken by the Johannine Epistles was not in vain. Imperfectly as the writer of 1J married the elements which, for a variety of reasons and from a variety of sources, came before him, his defence of the reality of the human Jesus as the way to God and his hold upon the unfinished yet hopeful nature of the moral struggle were two causes which it was vital to defend. It was also vital to insist, as he did, that the two could not be separated. In a wider way, his sense that brotherly love is the heart of ethics, while perhaps not controversial, was also a point which he did well to stress—even though for him the limits of its exercise may well have been narrow (cf. p. 120).

In these ways, the writer played a part in the ultimate securing of the work of the Johannine school of teaching in the early Church for the orthodox cause.

From another angle, we may see a kind of necessity for the stage in the development of Johannine affairs which these writings represent. Just as in the Pastoral Epistles we see the Pauline tradition adapting itself and applying itself to a situation where ecclesiastical and disciplinary considerations outweigh theological in prominence, so here we have a parallel moment in the Johannine churches. We may complain in both cases that, from the point of view of faithfulness to the original teaching (or the earlier examples of it that we possess), both attempts were inept or muddled. But if those traditions were to remain alive for the Church, the attempt had to be made—and to continue to be made. New applications of old teachings were essential, and in that process, both orthodox and heretics (as our writer virtually forces us to call them) played their part.

# INTRODUCTION: THE SITUATION

## NOTE ON THE RESURRECTION IN 1J

In connection with the doctrinal standpoint of the Johannine Epistles, one further factor merits discussion. While the death of Jesus is important (cf. e.g. i. 7; ii. 2), there are no references whatsoever to the resurrection (except indirectly perhaps in ii. 1, and there it is the results not the fact itself). The living Christ, in whom his people now dwell, is in the forefront of the writer's mind, but of the resurrection itself he is silent. Two comments are appropriate, both of them in the light of GJ.

First, there is a case for saying that in the Gospel, the resurrection, though it receives a good deal of attention (ii. 21 f.; xx–xxi), is, from a strictly doctrinal point of view, redundant. The Cross is the moment of Christ's glory (xiii. 31) and the consummation of his work (xix. 30). Both these ideas, in themselves more naturally associated with the resurrection or the second coming, are, by a creative stroke, transferred to the death. That is the moment of triumph and fulfilment.

Along another line of thought, however, there is one thing which the resurrection alone can add. Treated in a certain way, it adds 'solidity' to the Lord's 'fleshlyness'. GJ treats it in precisely this way: at first sight surprisingly in this Gospel, the risen Jesus is presented as one who can be touched (xx. 27), who cooks (xxi. 9) and perhaps eats (xxi. 12 f.), just as he also appears 'out of the air' (xx. 19, 26). We may not be far wrong in suggesting that this presentation serves the same purpose as that dear to the writer of 1J: to show that the saviour-Messiah and the human Jesus are one and the same. Admittedly, 1J does not carry this assertion beyond the death (v. 7, 'and the blood')—unless the variant in that verse ('and the Spirit') is indeed part of the original text and refers to the Lord's risen presence (as in GJ the Paraclete is in effect just that, xiv. 16-18), cf. p. 127 n. But if this is right, it explains the lack of explicit reference to the resurrection in 1–3J: its only point was to demonstrate Christ's humanity—which the writer has other ways of doing. And even if this was not so directly the major interest in the writing of GJ xx–xxi, those chapters may well have been taken thus by the writer of 1J, who is likely to have had other links, at least with GJ xxi; both seem to come from Johannine hands later than the writing of the body of GJ and to share a concern with authentic tradition.

We have written so far of the immediate situation in which the epistles originated, referring, as far as wider context is concerned, only to the earlier and later fortunes of Johannine teaching. But there is also the question of the remoter sources of the thought to which these writings bear witness. Is it possible to give definition to this group of Christians from connections between their ideas and those of other circles in the Church and world of the period?

But closely connected with this question is another which may suitably be considered first, as a way of entry to the other. It is the question of the structure of 1J.

## STRUCTURE

It is, after all, a puzzling work. No early Christian writing is so repetitious, so monotonous in its grammatical constructions, so narrow in vocabulary. The picture of the venerable elder, whom old age has endowed indeed with profundity of wisdom (Johannine fashion) but also with a natural incapacity to venture far in its formulation, is entirely understandable.

At times the argument approaches the circular, and drives scholars to look for muddles in the transmission of the text (e.g. v. 2). But it is better to describe the argument as a whole, in von Campenhausen's word (*Ecclesiastical Authority and Spiritual Power*, London, 1969, p. 186), as spiral; that is, while there is a circularity of movement involving a small number of ideas, there is also progression as new themes are introduced. At the same time, words are, from time to time, dropped after being central to the argument. But so small is the number of ideas in the writer's stock that they are usually replaced by other expressions which take over their role. Thus the contrast between light and darkness dominates the first part of the work, but neither word appears after ii. 11. On the other hand, the contrast between truth and falsehood occurs at intervals throughout the work. The idea of 'possessing' God or Christ is confined to ii. 23 and v. 12. The expression 'walk' (*peripateō*) for living the Christian life is found up to ii. 11 but never again. The verb 'to believe' does not appear before iii. 23 and is prominent chiefly in v. 1-13, just when expressions involving 'truth' (knowing it, being from it, having it in oneself) become rarer. 'Testimony' is confined to v. 9-11 (though the corresponding verb occurs twice before that passage, in rather stereotyped phrases, i. 2 and iv. 14). The idea of being 'born' from God does not occur until ii. 29, and then comes regularly through the rest of the work. It thus helps to form one of the replacements for the light–darkness contrast: those who are in the light are the same as those who are God's offspring, those in the darkness as the children of the devil. Similarly, to 'acknowledge' or 'confess' (*homologeō*) Jesus is the same as to believe (though it carries the additional idea of definite doctrinal affirmation), in the sense that both signify allegiance to God; but apart from ii. 23 it comes chiefly in ch. iv, whereas as we have seen 'believe' belongs to ch. v. 'Love', 'world', 'dwell' (or 'abide', *menō*) appear constantly (though the last is not in ch. v).

This phenomenon, together with the repetitious quality of the work, may be a clue to the mode of its composition—or (for it may be the better word) its assembly.

It is not always easy to tell where they begin and end, but the work seems to consist of a number of cycles of argument (apart from a prologue, i. 1-4, and, perhaps as an appendix, v. 13-21). As for example in the sections of Psalm 119, the number of genuinely distinct themes is very small—perhaps fundamentally only two: that belonging to God is his gift, and that those who possess it must live by the moral way which it demands, to wit, love of the Christian brothers. But the number of ways of expressing them is considerably greater and this makes possible the introduction of a number of dependent themes.

Each cycle includes a consideration of the central themes with some subordinate question in mind; or, alternatively, using the great, constant words and ideas for material, it radiates from some new notion or question, introduced or brought into prominence for the first time. In other words, it is like a series of connected, revolving discs, placed side by side, each of which differs from the rest in having a centre of distinctive colour. If the division between the sections is not always transparently clear (so that every commentator makes his own analysis), it is because the writer attempted to fuse them into a single whole, with varying degrees of success in concealing what lay behind. (So, for example, he introduces the idea of the Spirit, which dominates iv. 1-6, in iii. 24, which links two sections together.)

The sections may be as follows:

i. 5–ii. 11: centring on light and darkness.

ii. 12-17: a quite distinctive passage of solemn admonitions.

ii. 18-27: centring on denial and confession.

ii. 28-iii. 24: centring on membership of God's or the devil's family.

iv. 1-6: centring on the two kinds of spirits.

iv. 7-21: centring on the nature and demand of love.

v. 1-12: centring on victory and testimony.

Though his division differs, O'Neill (*The Puzzle of I John*, London, 1966, p.1) states the principle usefully: 'the progression of thought from one paragraph to the next is usually clear, but the thought of each paragraph usually runs parallel to that of a neighbouring paragraph, or to that of some other paragraph in the Epistle.'

At this point, a comparison with the structure of the Gospel is worth considering. A number of recent scholars (in particular R. E. Brown and Barnabas Lindars),[1] in examining the question of the process by which GJ was composed, have come to the conclusion that it was made up by joining together a number of episodes whose earlier formation took place independently, probably over a long period, in the context of the teaching and preaching of the Johannine congregation. This accounts both for their similarity in thought and vocabulary and for their lack of uniformity of structure, in particular in the way narrative and discourse are interrelated. The development of each episode has every sign of having been both long and complex. At the basis of each, there is usually a story or saying which is either the same as or very like a story or saying in one or more of the synoptic Gospels. But whereas in those Gospels stories or sayings were usually presented in brief or relatively simple form, the Johannine church worked in a different manner. Starting from the original kernel, they surrounded it with a whole web of reflective or homiletic theological material, reflecting a limited range of ideas, but using them and combining them in a wide variety of patterns. Hence the tantalizing similarity yet dissimilarity between the Gospel of John and the rest, and the presence of different kinds of similarity in different parts of the Gospel.

If this, or something like it, was the method used in forming the

[1] R. E. Brown, *The Gospel According to John, I–XII*, New York, 1966, pp. xxiv ff.; and Barnabas Lindars, *The Gospel of John*, London, 1972, and his shorter *Behind the Fourth Gospel*, London, 1971.

episodes which make up GJ, and if that Gospel resulted from the joining together of these episodes (with the addition of some extra sections, otherwise derived, and editorial matter), may an analogous procedure not lie behind the First Epistle? Here is another substantial, though more slender, product of the Johannine community, written at a crisis in its fortunes. It is less fine in its theological perception, less elaborate and varied in its thought, but it comes recognizably from the same stable. And it too, as we have seen, may be regarded as the result of putting together a number of discrete sections rather than of a single act of writing. As in the case of the Gospel, the sections will have their own distinct, though comparable, histories. As in the Gospel, there are many links of theme and vocabulary uniting many of the sections; but each has also its own colour, derived from the word or words upon which it focuses.

At this point, the question arises, is there in 1J anything corresponding to the kernel of story or saying which, according to the view we have represented, lies at the heart of the Gospel episodes? If there is, it is less obvious in this case, but it is possible that certain features of 1J may be explained by the presence of an element which plays this role. It would be a case of the Johannine church employing once more, in a different mode, a method which had already served it well over a long period of its existence.

One suggestion can be made on the basis of evidence provided by C. H. Dodd (Commentary, pp. xxxviii ff.). He points to a number of parallels between statements in 1J and sayings of Jesus found in the Gospels, chiefly that of Matthew. All have been 'johannized'—more thoroughly than such sayings found embedded in passages in GJ (e.g. xii. 25; cf. Matt. x. 39)—and some look like the products of mere coincidence; but it is not impossible that the sections of 1J developed like snowballs from a beginning in sayings of the kind found in the Gospels. Other ideas are, however, in the field.

There has been, over the past seventy years, a number of attempts to account for the diverse nature of the material in 1J by suggesting that behind it lies a shorter document which the writer took and elaborated, commenting on it in accordance with his own ideas and purposes. This diversity shows itself in two ways: most obviously in the matter of style, but also in the matter of tone. Right through 1J there are stripes consisting of neat, often antithetical propositions, starting typically with 'he who' or 'everyone who'—followed by some assertion (in Greek, using the present participle) about the nature of the Christian life or its opposite. These stripes alternate with sections which are more diffuse and less 'mandarin-like' in form and content—on the contrary, they are warm and pastoral; in the jargon, they manifest concern. The first kind of material is gnomic, almost proverbial, the second is hortatory and homiletic. The first often takes the form of bald statements which seem to take little account of practical problems (e.g. iii. 9; v. 18), the second is much more shaped to immediate needs (e.g. ii. 1 f.; v. 16). These two kinds of writing do not occur evenly or in sections of uniform length, any more than in the episodes of GJ the two elements of narrative and discourse are uniformly related to each other. In the various 'episodes' into which 1J may be divided, they appear in varying order and quantity.

The attempt to separate part at least of 1J into two elements began with the work of von Dobschütz ('Johanneische Studien, 1', *ZNW*, 8, 1907, pp. 1 ff.), who showed that in the passage ii. 29–iii. 10 can be found four antithetical and parallel pairs of statements,[1] themselves interrelated in sense, which have been filled out by other matter, less semitic (as von Dobschütz believed) and more rhetorical in form, less ethical in content and more concerned with the nature of existence.

More influential has been the complete analysis of 1J given by R. Bultmann in the *Festgabe für A. Jülicher* (Tübingen, 1927, republished in *Exegetica*, ed. E. Dinkler, Tübingen, 1967, pp. 105 ff.), entitled 'Analyse des ersten Johannesbriefes'. In his commentary, published in 1967, Bultmann made a few modifications to his work of forty years before, but in the main he reaffirmed his adherence to it, while acknowledging it as 'conjectural' (p. 23, n. 3). He discerned behind 1J a source consisting of twenty-six antithetical couplets (or triplets)—and one more is to be found in 2J 9. In the process of commenting on them and working them into the longer document, a number of the couplets may have been cut or altered, so that it is not possible to be sure whether certain lines, as they stand, are rightly assigned to this source or not.

[1] The six statements beginning 'everyone who' (*pas ho*) in ii. 29; iii. 4, 6, 9, 10, plus the pair in iii. 7 f.: 'he who does the right is righteous'—'he who commits sin springs from the devil'.

The source, consisting of aphorisms, apodictic in tone, is identifiable stylistically by the fact that the lines all have one of three openings: definite article + present participle ('he who e.g. loves'); the same preceded by *pas* ('everyone'); the conditional form ('if'—*ean*)—this last confined to i. 6-10 and iv. 12.

None of these aphorisms bears any strong marks of necessarily Christian origin. Though he modified this view in the commentary, Bultmann held in 1927 that the source was a work of pre-Christian, pagan Gnosis, and he believed it was related to the source from which the Johannine Christians derived the 'revelation' discourses in GJ. He was unimpressed by arguments that parallelism of structure signified in this case semitic origin.

The source has been filled out by the insertion of hortatory material, by which the editor made it serve his urgent need to correct the more extreme Gnosticism of the heretics. Whereas the source never gives reasons for its statements—it simply asserts—the editor's own work is characterized by the formula: 'by this we know'—which he uses nine times. It would be consistent with such a view to hold that the source was a work which, at least in part, both parties could respect and which was familiar to both. (But the heretics would not like i. 8 f., which Bultmann assigns to the source.) The pastorally minded editor sets out, by his use of it, to show its true bearing—just as Paul may have done in incorporating into his own work Col. i. 15-20, possibly a hymn well known to his opponents.

In a further essay on 1J ('Die kirchliche Redaktion des ersten Johannesbriefes', originally in essays *In Memoriam Ernst Lohmeyer*, Stuttgart, 1951, reprinted in *Exegetica*, ed. E. Dinkler, Tübingen, 1967, pp. 381 ff.), Bultmann suggested a refinement to his former analysis. An 'ecclesiastical redactor' was responsible for certain final but important touches to the writing which moved its message in the direction of 'ordinary' Church doctrine, using conventional formulae and ideas. It displays tendencies similar to those which may be ascribed to a similar final editing of GJ. They include the appendix, v. 14-21 (corresponding to ch. xxi in GJ), with its directions on penitential discipline—a distinctly 'churchy' topic; three statements of traditional eschatology, ii. 28; iii. 2; and iv. 17 (Bultmann takes ii. 18 to be not a sign that the End, as conventionally seen, is regarded as near, but as a statement of the doctrine that the End is realized already in the Church's present life—it is old Johannine teaching); and the references to Jesus' blood—again a popular Christian motif, but not readily assimilable to Johannine doctrine—in i. 7, where the phrase 'and the blood of Jesus his Son cleanses us from all sin' is an addition to the neat pattern of the source; also, finally, the similar references in ii. 2 and iv. 10b to Jesus as the sacrificial offering (*hilasmos*) for sin.

In his 1967 commentary, Bultmann adds one more feature to this picture. He suggests that i. 1–ii. 27 could easily have been the original work, to which has been added a set of Johannine pieces, none of which takes the argument significantly further. They are independent compositions on the same group of themes as the longer work, the product, it may be, of the work of disciples of the original writer.

This additional suggestion will strain the credulity of many, who will feel it improbable that such a short work had such a complex history; and Bultmann does little to relieve this sense when he states (Commentary, p. 48 n.) that his new idea 'has nothing to do with the source-analysis' which he had made so long before, and leaves it, apparently, essentially untouched.

While Bultmann's analysis has won wide acceptance, not everyone has agreed that the two chief elements which he distinguished spring from such different backgrounds. Both H. Braun (*ZThK*, 48, 1951, pp. 267–92) and W. Nauck, in his monograph, *Die Tradition und der Charakter des ersten Johannesbriefes* (Tübingen, 1957), questioned Bultmann's original conviction, which his commentary no longer upholds in its purity, that the source was of pre-Christian and pagan, Gnostic origin. It is too concerned with the forgiveness of sins (i. 9, the actual human acts, not 'sin', the cosmic power of evil) to come from a fully dualistic style of thought, too concerned with ways of life—walking in the light or in the darkness (i. 6–10), and with brotherly love (ii. 9–11), all signs of Jewish rather than pagan outlook. Nauck pointed to the close similarities of teaching (as distinct from manner and style) between source and editorial work, and held that both came from the same hand. (But what a strange procedure this is for a man to adopt with his own work!)

F. Büchsel, much earlier (*ZNW*, 20, 1929, pp. 235 ff.), shortly after the appearance of Bultmann's first work, held that even the separation into two elements was unjustifiable. There were parallels in Jewish literature to the movement from aphoristic to homiletic writing, as well as to the various patterns of antitheses in 1J, in particular in the Midrashim and the Pirke Aboth.[1] And as far as form was concerned, his point had force.

R. Schnackenburg, in his commentary (3rd ed. 1965), agreed that what lay behind the double nature of the material of 1J was not a source with added commentary but a duality of purpose: the writer had both to attack heretics and to encourage the faithful congregation. While the two purposes can be seen as fulfilled by the aphorisms and the hortatory material respectively, there is a considerable degree of overlap. And this very fact confirms the belief that we are dealing with a single work. Käsemann (*ZThK*, 48, 1951, p. 307) made the not dissimilar suggestion that it was a question not of two sources but of two kinds of tradition, which the writer used because they were suitable for his purposes; only Käsemann identifies them as Gnostic 'revelation' discourse and Christian homily.[2]

On any showing, 1J is nothing like as simple in structure as a straightforward alternation of neatly balanced antithetical aphorisms and hortatory comment: the two styles are mixed together and constantly the structure of the aphorisms has been spoiled, especially by introductory additions.

But whatever the objections, Bultmann's theory of two distinct backgrounds had the advantage of explaining without resorting to paradox the two minds apparent in 1J, especially on the subject of the sinfulness or sinlessness of Christians. In this commentary we have preferred to see a man caught in an unresolved dichotomy of thought and purpose rather than the use of two sources (see pp. 55 ff.). Those who adopt Bultmann's approach are left with the difficulty of explaining the final editor's failure to express a clear viewpoint: why did he use two sources yet lack the wit or the will to fuse their disparate teaching more satisfactorily?[3]

In the work of J. C. O'Neill (see p. 24), the idea of two distinct

---

[1] A collection of 'wisdom' sayings, roughly contemporary with the Johannine writings. Compare a saying like: Everyone who fulfils the Torah when poor will in the end fulfil it when rich; and everyone who makes it vain when rich will in the end make it vain when poor (PA iv. 11); with 1J v. 12 and iii. 9 f.

[2] For another useful critique of Bultmann's hypothesis, denying duality of source but claiming the use of traditional teaching, see O. A. Piper, '1 John and the Didache of the Primitive Church', *JBL*, 66, 1947, pp. 437 ff.

[3] Käsemann saw the inconsistency on post-baptismal sin as an example of the *simul iustus, simul peccator* principle, which Paul had worked out theologically, now receiving application in Church practice.

elements has been raised once more, but in a new guise, one that leads us on to the question of the theological affiliations of the epistle. He argues that 'the author of I John belonged to a Jewish sectarian movement, the bulk of whose members had become Christians by confessing that Jesus was the Messiah. The Epistle he wrote consists of twelve poetic admonitions belonging to the traditional writings of the Jewish movement; each of these he has enlarged in order to bring out the fact that it has reached its true fulfilment in the coming of Jesus. His opponents were the members of the Jewish sect who had refused to follow their brethren into the Christian movement.'[1] He sees in each of the twelve sections 'a clearly distinguishable source with a distinct poetic structure and a distinct pre-Christian theology' (p. 7), and finds that the editor then in his commentary enlarged 'his source in the interests of a defined Christian theology which takes account of the straining of loyalties which must have occurred if Jews, faithful to their own sect and its theology, had yet decided to accept Jesus as the fulfilment of their hopes' (p. 7).

This way of looking at 1J has the great merit of linking it with a known Christian practice, that of glossing and commenting upon existing Jewish texts. It also has the merit, more generally acceptable, even to those sceptical of the particular analysis, of showing that the theological background is Jewish. It places 1J among those many early Christian writings which, in a wide variety of ways, reflect the attempt to fix the boundary with Judaism and define the relationship between synagogue and church.

Any analysis of this writing is inevitably hypothetical. To say that O'Neill's work has this character is to make no damaging charge. More serious is its inadequacy in making it possible to relate 1J to GJ. We read only that 'John's Gospel…is probably a later development within the same tradition' (pp. 66 f.). Yet we have found many reasons for thinking that it is 1J which is the later work—a pastoral application of Johannine teaching at a time when institutional and disciplinary problems were much more pressing than at the time when the Gospel was written. The 'simpler' nature of the Epistle's theology (for example, its less elaborate christology and its more traditional eschatology) is by no means necessarily an argument for earlier date.

[1] p. 6. The twelve divisions are: i. 5-10; ii. 1-6; ii. 7-11; ii. 12-17; ii. 18-27; ii. 28–iii. 10a; iii. 10b-19a; iii. 19b-24; iv. 1-6; iv. 7-18; iv. 19–v. 13a; v. 13b-21.

Moreover, the allegedly Jewish oracles are full of words and expressions also found in GJ, and, though it is impossible to be sure, their use in the Epistle seems to take for granted their having already received that Christian and Johannine rooting which the Gospel gives to them. It is not merely a matter of vocabulary: the theology of many of the oracles, especially the centrality of the duty of brotherly love (admittedly paralleled in the Qumran sect) and the fact of the believer's abiding in God, is deeply Johannine. Is it not more likely that the units used in 1J are Johannine and Christian rather than Jewish and pre-Christian? Certainly, the answer turns more on the relationship between Epistle and Gospel than is allowed in O'Neill's work. The puzzle of 1J cannot be solved by attention to that writing alone.

But whether the process of composition was by the 'treating' of an underlying source or by direct writing, it seems more useful to suppose that 1J consists of a series of independent sections, bound together with varying degrees of smoothness and with additions giving the outward semblance of a single composition, than to try to find a single logical thread. Insistence on the latter approach is liable to lead to infinite complexity or to despair.

Reverting to the division suggested earlier (pp. 23 f.), we find that each of these sections, except ii. 12-17 and iv. 1-6, includes aphorisms ascribed by Bultmann to the source. Also, each of them except ii. 12-17 and ii. 18-27 includes at least one of the passages which use the formula 'By this we know', which J. A. T. Robinson (*Twelve New Testament Studies*, London, 1962, p. 127) has called 'tests by which (the readers) may assure themselves of the Christian position'. In fact, ii. 18-27 does contain statements of a comparable character (e.g. ii. 27). Is there then not much to be said for the view that the main sections of 1J are a set of homiletic pieces, using accepted maxims of the congregation (which may have existed in a formal, though only loosely continuous, collection), and applying them, by means of cogent, pointed additions, to two issues—the nature of Christian allegiance, and the specific form in which that matter was being urgently raised by the rise of disagreement to the point of schism (ii. 19) in the church? Many of the maxims use ideas already employed in GJ, some of them (e.g. i. 8-10) do not.

1J is then not a letter, it is a theological tract, modelled roughly on this congregation's existing production, GJ, especially in structure and terminology, and in the use and contents of the prologue. This is not to say that 1J does not have one or two features which give it something of the appearance of a letter which has lost top and tail: there are thirteen occurrences of the verb 'write' (*graphō*), chiefly in expressions like 'I have written to you' (e.g. v. 13). Six of them are concentrated in ii. 12-14, a passage which on any showing is likely to lack a pre-history. The statements where this word occurs probably all belong, as they stand, to the final stage of composition. GJ itself contains elements of similar direct personal address to the reader (xix. 35; xx. 30 f.; xxi. 24 f.). The underlying sectional structure puts 1J alongside GJ; and if there was ever a separate 'book of signs', a collection of homiletically developed stories of Jesus' acts, before the full Gospel shape was reached, then the similarity would be even closer.

In the Epistle, the purpose was not to bring faith (as in the Gospel, xx. 31), but to bring renewed conviction to believers now under pressure from what the writer is convinced is seriously erroneous teaching (1J v. 13). And the dominant contrast is no longer, as in the Gospel, between God's revelation and the world, but between true doctrine and false. The conflict now is not only around the Church but also within its borders.

## THEOLOGICAL AFFINITIES

Whereas, as we have seen, it was possible and fashionable in former days to seek the background of Johannine thought in the contemporary religious world of Greek paganism, it is clear that the heterodox and often highly speculative Jewish theology of the time affords closer parallels. The distinction is by no means absolute: Jewish theology itself in this period was deeply influenced by the orientalized Hellenism of the day. But it is the narrower rather than the wider scene which is determinative for our Epistles. If we make our approach from this standpoint, we shall find that it illuminates not only the thought of the writer but also that of the opponents with whom he contends.

The factor which has chiefly shifted the balance of probability in this matter is the increased knowledge of contemporary Jewish sectarian thought through the discovery of the Dead Sea Scrolls. It is notable that Bultmann, so long attached to the Gnostic view of at least major sources of Johannine thought, moved, in his 1967 commentary, firmly in the direction indicated by the new evidence. He refers to the close parallels between 1J and the Qumran writings, and while he rejects O'Neill's thesis, he recognizes (p. 11) that 1J presupposes the tradition of Jewish language and thought. While he can continue to hold (p. 23, n. 1) that 'Johannine dualism has its roots not in the Old Testament but in Gnosis', he sees this as mediated through the existing influence of Gnosis on Judaism, as evidenced in (among other places) the Dead Sea Scrolls.

The most striking similarity between 1J and DSS is the strongly dualistic framework of thought which they share, and which is expressed in either identical or closely similar terms (light and darkness, truth and error or sin). In both, it is not a question of explicit cosmological dualism where two contrary powers face each other (but cf. p. 73); it is more a question of a moral division in the human will, in 'the world' which is its sphere of action and where indeed the wickedness of man rules. Light and darkness are opposing spheres of moral action, or 'walking' (i. 6 f.). The two kinds of men, children of God and of the devil (ii. 28 ff.), and the two kinds of spirits (iv. 1-6) substantiate the comparison. So does the figure—closely related to the Spirit—of the community's spokesman or advocate, in GJ identified with the Spirit of truth, in 1J with Jesus, the teacher and leader of the community. So too do the more practical aspects of the theology of 1J: its concern with the disciplining of the members of the community and with the grading of sins (v. 16 f.), its interest in sin as 'lawlessness' (iii. 4), its giving of prominence to brotherly love among the members of the community (iii. 16 f.), and its strong sense of the division between those inside and those outside its frontiers. (For a full account see ed. J. H. Charlesworth, *John and Qumran*, London, 1972, especially the essays by James L. Price and Marie-Émile Boismard.)

In the light of the background, what are we to make of the controversy of which 1J is the result? How are we to define the heretics? It has been alleged that they are pagan Gnostics, who cannot admit that any effective saviour could have come 'in the flesh', for 'flesh' is hopelessly corrupt (iv. 2; 2J 7). They are Gnostics too because they see salvation as conferring upon them a charmed existence, a miraculous immunity from sin (i. 8 ff.), to the extent, it may be, that actions of theirs, however immoral in everybody else's eyes, *cannot* be sins (cf. H. Jonas, *The Gnostic Religion*, Boston, 1958, pp. 270 ff.): yet, in the writer's eyes, they are guilty of the deepest sin in their failure to love (that is, among other things, continue to adhere to) their fellow-Christians. They have 'gone out from' them (ii. 19), thereby showing their true nature. It is their chief failure that they cannot see that redeemed status entails—and is recognizable by—the carrying out of stringent moral obligations.

It has been alleged on the other hand that they are Jews. The question at issue in 1J is whether, in the person of Jesus, the Messiah has come. Only Jews would be interested in such a question. This view has recently been stated cogently by J. C. O'Neill and J. A. T. Robinson (op. cit.). (See ii. 22–iii. 1, and, using the title Son of God, cf. p. 116, iv. 15; v. 5.)

Is there any way of combining the data on which these two contrary hypotheses base themselves and perhaps taking account of other features of the heresy which may be gleaned from 1J?

We may discount at the outset the complaint made by the writer against the heretics that they neglect brotherly love: no doubt it was a legitimate charge, but moral failure is not a monopoly of the heretics, as i. 8–ii. 2 and v. 16 f. make plain—the sinfulness of undoubted members of the true community of God's children is one of our writer's chief problems. And if the measure of this sin is failure to love the 'orthodox', then no doubt the 'heretics' could have brought a comparable charge with equal justice, and 1J might have been part of the evidence. Still, the failure to link theology and morals in a single system of thought may well be a weakness of their teaching: they were, for preference, speculators and intellectuals rather than men of action, and we have suggested (p. 15) that cloudiness of mind was perhaps one of their most powerful arguments against the old Johannine teaching as represented by the orthodox.

But on the issue of Jesus, where precisely was the difficulty? We suggest that it was not a difficulty over belief that the Messiah had come, but an inability to credit that he was to be identified from start to finish (from the water of his baptism to the blood of his death, v. 6) with the man Jesus. The emphasis in passages like v. 1 and iv. 15 is not that Jesus is *the Messiah* or *the Son of God*, but that *Jesus* (yes, Jesus) is the Messiah or the Son of God. The heretics believe that the Messiah has come and has acted effectively

—this they have in common with those from whom they have now separated; and the great theological assertions in 1J about the status of believers are no doubt statements which formerly, when they were a single community, both groups could rehearse together. Indeed, the fact that they could so plausibly be ascribed to a Gnostic source indicates that the creative theological work which they represent—together with GJ to which they are often so similar—owes more to those who have gone into schism than to the conservatives who are left behind. What the heretics cannot accept is that the Messiah, whose visitation has had such spectacular results (such as the gifts of eternal life and sinlessness for his followers), is at all points identical with the human Jesus who had suffered death.

The conservatives are reactionaries. They have come to feel, perhaps more in their bones than in their heads, that 'things were going too far' (2J 9), and they have turned back. Yet they have failed to assimilate adroitly their new thoughts (which are old thoughts) to their existing—and still affirmed—theological framework. So traditional eschatological feeling has been revived and finds expression (iv. 17) alongside statements which breathe the old Johannine atmosphere, the conviction of living already in the new age. Those high formulations concerning Jesus' person and role (above all the 'I am' sayings) which are the theological core of GJ are abandoned in favour of more commonplace and simple ways of speaking of him: in practice, everything turns on his being entitled to be called Messiah. It is as if other expressions are either agreed, or, more likely, dangerously speculative, or else somewhat beyond our more pedestrian writer (but cf. iv. 15). And where there is an attempt to imitate the high christology of GJ, as in i. 1-4, it is quite unclear how much is being claimed but it looks very much as if Jesus is esteemed for his message rather than his 'being' or his 'nature'. Yet the clearly crucial assertion that in Jesus the Messiah came 'in the flesh' (iv. 2) is never properly explained. There is no full-dress theology to answer the doubtless elaborate teaching of the heretics concerning their purely spiritual, angel-like Messiah.

The nearest we get to such an explanation is probably in convictions related to the statements that God is love (iv. 8), and that this is authenticated by the sending of his Son into the world which lies in the power of the Evil One (v. 19). This lies so close to our writer's heart that surely it moved him most deeply as he saw where one must take one's stand. The daring mission of the Son of God was an act of astonishing love precisely because it was a coming 'in the flesh'. It effected salvation 'out of the world'— that was agreed by orthodox and heretics alike—but what mattered was that it was an act of love on this scale (iii. 16). It was the making of contact between God and man, for man's salvation. The orthodox was moved to see it even more in its moral than in its soteriological aspect. It was salvation, yes, but it was also a spur to action: it constituted a demand to bodily, 'fleshly' kindness to one's brother, and the miraculous love of God was its source.

If the quarrel was about the person of the Messiah, and if there was, as it appears, agreement to believe that the Messiah had come, then surely this was not a dispute between Jews and Christians or between Jewish converts to Christianity and the Jews of their sect whom they had left behind or between ex-Jewish and ex-pagan Christians, but between factions in a Christian— albeit a Jewish-Christian—congregation.[1] The heretics are those who have taken a few, no doubt crucial, steps beyond the main position represented by GJ, and in so doing have provoked a reaction. So that the rest have taken steps backward—or side-ways—towards the common teaching of other, probably stronger and more influential Christian groups. The heretics, no doubt feeling themselves to be the authentic guardians and exponents of the Johannine teaching, have gone into schism in order to maintain it in its purity and clarity. In that claim they may well have had much to be said in their favour.

Their kind of Christian faith, with its belief in a spiritual angelic saviour, is by no means unparalleled in the speculation of contemporary Judaism (cf. e.g. Charlesworth, op. cit., p. 149), nor is it hard to find other examples of Christians who shared this approach. Cerinthus is commonly and fairly cited as a good example of such teaching. Active in just our period, he distin-

---

[1] GJ is interested in the mission to the Gentiles: xii. 20 ff., 32. But the three Epistles give no hint of the Church's dual composition—Jews and Gentiles. It is impossible to tell whether this is because the incorporation of Gentiles into the community is taken for granted and no longer an issue, or whether for these Christians it has never become a practical question. If there are non-Jewish members of the Johannine church, their theological influence remains in the background.

guished between the man Jesus and the divine Messiah who dwelt in him from his baptism until just before his death (cf. 1J v. 6 as an attack, possibly, on views such as this); and Cerinthus was a Jew. The men of Qumran believed in angelic leaders who would fight on their behalf (Charlesworth, op. cit., pp. 163 f.), though both groups in 1J would, if we are right, differ from this view in that for them the saviour had already carried out his mission. The two groups agreed further that he had done it in relation to Jesus, but for the heretics he had not identified himself with Jesus to the full, nor had he offered himself in death as a sacrificial victim for man's sin (ii. 2; iv. 10). (For further evidence of comparable contemporary thought, this time on the basis of 'wisdom' teaching, in the Odes of Solomon, see J. T. Sanders, *The New Testament Christological Hymns*, Cambridge, 1971, pp. 104 ff.)

We have found that the answers to the questions from which we began have intermingled (p. 1). Each has contributed to a total picture of the nature and significance of the three Epistles. Though they are not among the most important remains of early Christianity, they still throw light on an important stage in its development, both theologically and institutionally. They show the strengths and even more the weaknesses of the resources which Christians had at their disposal as they set out to stabilize their faith and their Church in the years that followed the earliest missions. At a time when, as we can see from other writings, the temptation was to take refuge in authority rather than thought, the First Epistle at least shows an admirable determination to let the truth as its writer sees it continue to speak for itself and carry conviction, if possible, by its inherent power.

### NOTE ON THE COMMON AUTHORSHIP OF THE GOSPEL AND FIRST EPISTLE

The question of the common authorship of the two major Johannine writings is still much disputed. Most recent writers speak in terms of a 'Johannine school', responsible for both works. Few now assert identity of authorship throughout, but many scholars are prepared to see the hand of the writer of the Epistle at work at certain points (perhaps at a late stage) in the composition of the Gospel. Some, notably R. Schnackenburg (Commentary, pp. 34 ff.), feel the nicely balanced state of the question: features often reckoned to exclude identity of authorship can mostly be laid at the door of the differences of literary form and external circumstances.

There are two kinds of argument, stylistic and, in the widest sense, circumstantial. With regard to style and vocabulary, the case against identity of authorship is stated by C. H. Dodd, in *BJRL*, 21, 1937, pp. 129 ff., and the contrary case by W. F. Howard, *JTS*, 48, 1947, pp. 12 ff. and W. G. Wilson, *JTS*, 49, 1948, pp. 147 ff. The evidence is summarized in Kümmel, *Introduction to the New Testament*, London, 1966, p. 311. If this approach seems inconclusive, a consideration of the thought and purpose of the two works points more plainly to the view that they are unlikely to come from the same hand. They share many ideas, but the differences are of such a character as to indicate that the Epistle represents a time when Johannine thought had developed in new directions since the writing of the Gospel. New problems had arisen for solution, chiefly in relation to authority and right faith. Above all, though the Epistle is deeply theological, there is a shift of emphasis from the doctrinal to the ecclesiastical and the pastoral. Despite the relative simplicity and (a quality hard to judge) primitiveness of some of the teaching of the Epistle, it is difficult not to believe that these concerns indicate a later date and a different hand. This is the view taken in this book.

## HISTORY AND ACCEPTANCE

The First Epistle is quoted by writers of main-stream Christianity some decades before the Johannine Gospel. This may reflect, if not actual knowledge on their part that 1J was, in relation to GJ, a conservative modification of Johannine thought, at least a feeling that it was a 'safer' document. In that case, our writer succeeded in the design we have ascribed to him—to safeguard the Johannine teaching for 'orthodoxy' at a time when others were developing it, to his mind treacherously, in a Gnostic direction. If it was another of his objects to stamp GJ as 'orthodox' (perhaps by 'touching it up', cf. p. 12), then, to judge from the absence of reference to which we have referred, in this he was less successful. Whether either work was already linked with the authority-giving name of John (Apostle or Elder) we cannot tell.

All this is speculation, even if it has a certain plausibility. The evidence, after all, for this early 'orthodox' use of 1J is meagre.

Still, one piece of it, that in the Epistle to the Philippians by Polycarp, bishop of Smyrna, who died *c.* A.D. 156, merits careful discussion in relation to our general picture.

In the first place, Polycarp had links with 'John'—whether the Apostle or not is unclear. The evidence comes from Irenaeus who knew him (died *c.* A.D. 200), by way of the fourth-century Eusebius (*Ecclesiastical History* v. 20. 6), quoting original sources. In the second place, Polycarp is noticeably Johannine in thought and language. How strange then that, like his contemporary Justin, his work contains no quotation from GJ (he has a number from Paul), no appeal to its authority. In fact that work does not appear among 'the Gospels' until the end of the second century—in Irenaeus and the Roman church's Muratorian Canon; before that it is known only as a possession of the Valentinian Gnostics (cf. p. 11).

Let us now place the situation with regard to Polycarp alongside the development in the Johannine community which, we have suggested, may lie behind the NT writings which stem from it. Polycarp's defensiveness about the Johannine Gospel (if that is what it is) accords well with its having been effectively 'taken over' by Christians of a Gnostic outlook who interpreted it in a way which went beyond its writer's intentions, coming down on one side of certain doctrinal fences which he sat, perhaps uneasily, astride.[1] Nevertheless, the Johannine way of formulating the Christian faith has not been monopolized by these men, even if they are perhaps its most striking exponents. From the start, there was an 'orthodox' Johannine wing: 1J was its first literary production, and Polycarp may well stand in its tradition. (And, for what it is worth, Irenaeus associates his Christian allegiance with the name of John—which of course appears nowhere in the actual text of those writings which the NT canon came to ascribe to him.[2])

If Polycarp refrains from quoting the Gospel (supposing that he knew of it), he confirms our reconstruction by alluding directly to 1J. In ch. vii of his Epistle, he writes: 'To deny that Jesus Christ has come in the flesh is to be Antichrist. To contradict the evidence of the Cross is to be of the devil' (*ECW*, p. 147). He could have given no clearer signal that he stands in the tradition of the

[1] Cf. S. S. Smalley, 'Diversity and Development in John', *NTS*, 17, 1971. The 'fences' concern chiefly eschatology and attitude to the created order.

[2] On this whole question, see J. N. Sanders & B. A. Mastin, *The Gospel According to St. John*, London, 1968, pp. 32 ff.

conservative Johannine reaction which, we believe, the writer of
1J represents. For he mentions no less than four of its distinctive
points: that Jesus Christ has come in the flesh (cf. 1J iv. 2); that
to deny this is so serious as to be a sign of the devil's activity (ii.
22); that the reality of Jesus' death as Messiah ('the cross') is the
acid test of belief that he came in the flesh (v. 6); and that this
belief is the only authentic faith ('let us...turn back again to the
word which was delivered to us from the beginning', Polycarp,
*Phil.* vii. 2; cf. 1J i. 1; ii. 24).

How much later Polycarp is writing than the author of 1J himself is uncertain. The consensus of opinion is that this part of the
Epistle dates from *c.* A.D. 135.[1] If GJ is to be dated, as most
scholars now believe, at the turn of the century, the Johannine
Epistles may come about mid-way between the two dates.

The only other early reference is not inconsistent with this,
though it is more shadowy and so less valuable. Eusebius (III. 39.
17) says that Papias, bishop of Hierapolis and a contemporary
of Polycarp, used 'the former epistle of John'. If accurate (and
Eusebius had the works of Papias before him), this is evidence for
the existence not only of 1J but also of at least one other Epistle.
(In the Greek of the period, 'former' need not imply that there
were only two.)

Ignatius of Antioch, writing at about the time we suggest for
the Epistles, faced (cf. *Smyrneans* vii, *ECW*, p. 121) some of the
same doctrinal issues as their author, and he takes his stand on the
same ground; but there is nothing in either writer to indicate
knowledge of the other's work, despite converging lines of thought.

If then 1J at least was in existence and seen as worth quoting
before the middle of the second century, its wider acceptance was
assured by that century's close. Irenaeus quotes it (and 2J) and
attributes both works to 'John, the Lord's disciple' (*Adversus
Haereses* I. 9. 3; III. 17. 5, 8). By this time, 1J was recognized
further afield, away from the area, Asia Minor, with which the
Johannine tradition was particularly linked. Clement of Alexandria
quotes 1J and knows it as the work of John the Apostle. And in the
West too, acceptance has now come—of GJ as well as of the
Epistles. This must have been rather more of a victory for the
Johannine cause: the Alexandrian church's combination of ortho-

---

[1] P. N. Harrison, *Polycarp's Two Epistles to the Philippians*, London, 1936;
especially pp. 300 f.

doxy and Platonism made these writings especially congenial, but this attraction did not apply in Rome. It is almost certainly a sign of the power of an apostolic name in the Roman church and so of the firmness with which 'John' was now seen as the writer of these works. This was the belief which achieved their rescue from the Gnostic camp—especially in those circles for which their terminology and thought had no special doctrinal attractiveness.

Acceptance by the Roman church is testified in the Muratorian Canon, *c.* A.D. 200 (Stevenson, pp. 144 ff.). The meaning of the passage concerned is not wholly clear. After speaking of the Fourth Gospel, it quotes 1J i. 1 as evidence of John's testimony; then, at the conclusion of an account of Acts and the Pauline Epistles, it says: *epistola sane Jude et superscripti*[1] *Iohannis duas in catholica habentur.* Accepting *duas* as vulgar Latin for *duae*, the translation is usually taken to be: 'Certainly the epistle of Jude and two of the aforementioned John are held in the Catholic Church.' But, as Peter Katz has pointed out (*JTS*, 8, 1957, pp. 273 f.), the document refers to the Church elsewhere as *ecclesia catholica* and the use of the adjective alone in this sense would be strange. Moreover, the mention of two Epistles only when 2J and 3J seem such an inseparable pair (but see above concerning Irenaeus' use of 1J and 2J alone) inspires the attempt to arrive at a better understanding of the meaning of the sentence. The Muratorian fragment was translated from Greek and the presence of an error in the very next clause led Katz to suggest an emendation. Taking *catholica* as short for *epistola catholica*, 'catholic epistle' (as commonly), he suggests that *in* represents, mistakenly, the Greek *sun*, in the sense of 'in addition to'. The meaning then is: '...of the aforementioned John two in addition to the catholic (i.e. 1J) are held.' If this were correct, it would be the earliest sure evidence for the knowledge and recognition of three Johannine epistles. (C. F. D. Moule, *The Birth of the NT*, London, 1962, p. 206 n., reaches the same sense, but suggests the Greek preposition may have been *pros*, more naturally leading to Latin *in*.)

How 3J, particularly, escaped oblivion is an unanswered question. It is not only brief like 2J, but also devoid of material useful in doctrinal controversy. Surely its interest was fleeting.

---

[1] The Milan manuscript reads *superscrictio*. Did the writer intend *superscriptae*, to agree with *duae* (*epistolae*), or *superscripti*, to agree with *Iohannis*? We suppose the latter.

Like Philemon, also of largely personal concern (cf. J. Knox, *Philemon among the Letters of Paul*, London, 1960), it may have survived either because of early association with an apostolic figure, or because of its peculiar value to men in a position to preserve it. In the latter case, we may suppose that the quarrel to which it bears witness ate deep into the heart of the Johannine church and that the memory of it was preserved in its annals long enough for the former factor to begin to play an important, if not necessarily undisputed, part.

## NOTE ON THE JOHANNINE COMMA

Some time in the third century, at a time when the doctrine of the Trinity was being elaborated and was beginning to be in the forefront of many Christian minds, certain Latin interpreters of 1J seized upon the threefold reference in v. 7, 'the Spirit, the water and the blood'. They saw in it a providential springboard for the understanding of the text, and formed words like these (there were variations) to express it: 'There are three that bear witness on earth, the Spirit, the water and the blood, and these three are one. And there are three who bear witness in heaven, the Father, the Word and the Spirit.' The earliest clear witness to its actual inclusion is in a quotation from 1J by Priscillian, the Spanish heretic who died in A.D. 385. But other writers discerned this edifying and rhythmically attractive meaning in the text: the north Africans, Cyprian and then Augustine. Tertullian too hovered close, cf. *De Baptismo* 6. Perhaps this was where the idea started, and Cyprian (*De Unitate* 6) may even have had it in his text of 1J (cf. W. Thiele, *ZNW*, 50, 1959, pp. 61–73). If he did, then its insertion is carried back to the third century in the African church, perhaps even earlier.

It is unknown in the Greek manuscript tradition before the twelfth century, and in the Latin tradition (on which the Greek here depends) before the eighth century. From then on its prevalence in the West grew until its inclusion was accepted. At the Reformation, scholars like Erasmus tried to remove it, but tradition was too strong. It survived in the Vulgate and in the Authorized Version, and only relatively recently has disappeared into the margin or entirely. (*Komma* = section, Gk.)

To make a first acquaintance with the most important works on the Johannine Epistles, the problems raised and the solutions propounded, see W. Kümmel, *Introduction to the NT*, London, 1966. Then, for an exhaustive bibliography, see the commentary of R. Schnackenburg (details below), pp. xi–xxi; and for an equally exhaustive survey of the content of the relevant literature, showing how scholarly opinion has developed, see E. Haenchen, 'Neuere Literatur zu den Johannesbriefen', *ThR*, 26, 1960, pp. 1–43, 267–91.

General orientation may usefully start from W. Bauer, *Orthodoxy and Heresy in Earliest Christianity*, London, 1972 (German edition, 1934); and H. von Campenhausen, *Ecclesiastical Authority and Spiritual Power*, London, 1969; then, directly on the Epistles, turn to W. Marxsen, *Introduction to the NT*, Oxford, 1966, sections 25 & 26; J. A. T. Robinson, *Twelve NT Studies*, London, 1962, no. IX; E. Schweizer on 'The concept of the church in the gospel and epistles of St John', in ed. A. J. B. Higgins, *NT Essays* (presented to T. W. Manson), Manchester, 1959. In this field, there are also two influential German articles, H. Conzelmann, 'Was von Anfang war', in *NT Studien für R. Bultmann*, Beiheft 21 zur *ZNW*, 1957, pp. 194–201; and E. Käsemann, 'Ketzer und Zeuge', *ZThK*, 48, 1951, pp. 292–311, also to be found in his collected *Exegetische Versuche und Besinnungen*, I, 1960, pp. 168–87 (for an account of this article in English, see W. Bauer, op. cit., p. 308). For Jewish links, see *John and Qumran*, ed. J. H. Charlesworth, London, 1972.

The main literature on the structure of the First Epistle is listed and discussed on pp. 26 ff.; that on the relationship of the First Epistle and the Gospel of John on pp. 37 f.

Commentaries: in English, in order of date the list of significant works comes to an end with that of C. H. Dodd, 1946 (Moffatt NT Commentary). Before that in the present century, the notable commentaries are those by B. F. Westcott, 1908, and A. E. Brooke, 1912 (in the International Critical Commentary, a mine of detailed information). There is also the more diffuse R. Law, *The Tests of Life*, 1909.

In German, there are two important recent commentaries: the long and detailed work by R. Schnackenburg (*Die Johannesbriefe*,

Freiburg, 1st ed. 1953, 3rd ed. 1965) and the incisive, crisp and brief commentary by R. Bultmann in the Meyerkommentar (*Die drei Johannesbriefe*, Göttingen, 1967), which should be read alongside his earlier articles, cf. pp. 26 f. See review of Bultmann by D. Moody Smith in *JBL*, 88, 1969, pp. 120 f.

In French, there are the elegant commentary by A. Loisy,[1] to be found in the second edition of *Le Quatrième Évangile* (1921, pp. 530 ff.), and the brief work by J. Bonsirven (*Verbum Salutis*, Paris, 1954).

Works of reference and articles on detailed points are referred to in the commentary in the appropriate place.

[1] Interestingly listed by Schnackenburg, p. xv, under modern Protestant commentaries!

# THE FIRST EPISTLE OF JOHN

## 1. THE WORD OF LIFE
### i. 1-4

**(1) That which existed from the beginning—that which we heard, that which we saw with our own eyes, that which we gazed upon and our own hands felt—concerning the word of life; (2) and that life was revealed, and we saw and we testify and we announce eternal life to you. It was with the Father and was revealed to us. (3) What we saw and heard, we announce to you, yes, to you, so that you too may share our fellowship. This fellowship of ours is with the Father and with his Son, Jesus Christ. (4) We are writing this to make our joy complete.**

If these words were the opening of a spoken piece, we might accept them without too much difficulty as the language of ecstasy, the utterance of one in a state of high religious feeling. It is hard to take this view of them when they come before us as the opening words of a literary work. In that role they can only be described as, formally at least, bordering on incoherence. Yet it is scarcely fair to draw this distinction so sharply; or rather, having drawn it, we are compelled to recognize a duality which is to be found not only in this work but also in a number of other early Christian writings.

There is on the one hand an undeniable crudity of expression: I John certainly discloses itself in this respect at the very start. It never aspires to literary heights, though never again does it lapse into grammatical impossibilities. On the other hand, there is throughout this work a striking intensity of religious concentration. The writer is occupied with a small number of thoughts which he feels to be of the profoundest significance and which he presents again and again. The manner of these opening verses is then typical of the whole work.

In content too these verses are characteristic. Whether or not they were written as an introduction, when the rest was complete, they suitably foreshadow what is to come. The idea of seeing and testifying recurs in iv. 14 and v. 6 ff., and we find the factual nature of Christian origins reaffirmed in iv. 2 and v. 6. The prominence of this theme right at the start confirms—if confirmation were needed—how central it is for this writer. And quite apart from an analysis of the structure of the work (cf. p. 23), the voicing of this central theme in the opening statement is enough to justify our thinking of these verses as a prologue to the work as a whole.

Intensity of soul does not mean clarity of mind; and the grammatical incoherence is not compensated by immediate intelligibility. We cannot take these verses and say: You express yourself oddly, but I see that this is what you aim to tell us. In this respect, these verses are not typical of most of the rest of 1J. For the most part (with the exception of one or two notorious inconsistencies) the thought is clear enough. So in this way the introduction stands apart, and this may be used as an argument for its having come from an editorial hand, less skilful than the simple but on the whole unconfused composer of the main work. And any theory of the make-up of 1J which sees it as a collection of much used and so polished products of the Johannine church, adapted, no doubt, to fit into a connected whole and to serve specific needs, has no need to be surprised at the contrast between the prologue and the rest, cf. pp. 23 ff.

The problem of the independence of this section cannot be solved without looking ahead to i. 5. The words **message** (*angelia*), **announce,** and **heard** echo the prologue and can easily be read as the writer's final, successful attempt to 'get out' what he has been struggling to express for several lines. But they may also be read as editorial work, smoothing the transition from the prologue to the opening of the first main section, with its key pronouncement that **God is light**.

However immediate his link with the rest of the work, or with certain elements within it, the writer of these verses appears to have attempted to model himself upon the prologue of the Johannine Gospel. Yet the two passages are related in such a way that it is scarcely credible that the same man wrote both. Indeed the relationship between these two introductions is surely one of the strongest arguments against identity of authorship, if not throughout the two works, then at least in the production of these passages.

Much of i. 1-4 is reminiscent of GJ i. 1-18, yet the divergences are as significant as the similarities.

Theologically, the 1J passage lacks the profundity of the Gospel parallel. Whether the idea of the Word in GJ is philosophically elaborate or not, it is maintained with a certain rigour throughout the passage (though with interruptions), and clearly stands for Christ in his mediatorial role. In 1J, however, it is quite unclear whether **the word of life** (*v.* 1) refers to Christ or the Gospel message. It is as if the writer knows some of the words of the Gospel's prologue (especially *v.* 14), but has not absorbed its thought, finding it more congenial to work with simpler ideas (as other evidence also suggests, cf. p. 14). Similarly, in *v.* 4, if **this** refers to 1J as a whole, and if there is conscious dependence upon GJ xv. 11 and xvi. 24, then the sense of the expression **to make our joy complete** is altered if not trivialized. In GJ the joy in question is the profound satisfaction to be gained from participation in that eternal life which the Son has come to bestow on those who belong to him. Here it refers simply to the writer's hope to achieve his desired objectives as a result of his writing. And even if the text originally read 'your joy', the sense would gain little in depth.

Not only is the theology both muddier and shallower than in the Gospel, but the whole perspective is different. This cannot be put down to the same writer's having changed purpose and literary genre. It looks much more like the result of a new Christian generation with new problems to solve and pressures to endure. This passage is not, like the Gospel prologue, concerned primarily with the person and role of Christ the Word: whatever other, possibly polemical, motives are at work there, e.g. concerning the Baptist, they are subordinate to this central theme. But our passage is concerned to establish authenticity of witness to Christ. It is an assertion of credentials, made on the basis of an appeal to the past. Factuality and the past: these concerns stand to the fore here to a degree unknown in the Gospel.

This ranges 1J alongside a number of other writings, all of which bear witness to early attempts to establish criteria of Christian authority and, implicitly, to the rise of doctrinal diversity within the Church: in particular the Acts of the Apostles with its picture of unalloyed, exemplary harmony in the Church's first years, and the Pastoral Epistles with their passion for orthodoxy.

This motif is hardly visible in GJ—with any clarity only in the appendix, xxi. 20 ff., which is likely to be another later product of Johannine Christianity. The other works we have mentioned all spring from circles which held Paul's name in veneration. Both Pauline and Johannine circles were then beginning to be compelled, about the turn of the first century, to come to terms with the disturbing phenomena of sharp doctrinal conflict, division and heresy. The incoherence of the opening of 1J is symbolic of the bewildering and perplexing nature of the challenge.

The clearest evidence that this is the standpoint of 1J is the opening set of four clauses, each beginning **that which**. The reader is immediately reminded of GJ i. 14—the two passages have the verb *etheasametha* (**we gazed upon**): but the thrust is quite changed. In both cases, **we** refers not to the writer as an individual or with his associates but rather to the common Christian mind. Yet there is a difference. In the Gospel **we** seems to represent all believers, identifying themselves with those who first saw and believed. But here[1] in 1J, **we** are distinct from **you**. It is a case of responsible leaders addressing the rest, and it is the former who identify themselves with the first eyewitnesses. Moreover, the words **we gazed upon** no longer express, as in the Gospel, the response of faith to the saving appearance of the Word in the world; rather, they take their place alongside the other verbs to assert the reality of that appearance. This is not only a theological statement, it is a manifesto. Whereas the Gospel concentrates on the person of Christ, the introduction to 1J is more concerned with the fact and content of orthodox belief: the four clauses start with the neuter pronoun—**that which**—not the personal 'whom'.

H. Conzelmann (op. cit., pp. 194 ff.) has suggested that the word **beginning** is part of this picture, and is another aspect of the difference between the Gospel and the Epistle. In contemporary Jewish and Christian usage, it was a word of great sonority and mystery. Its occurrence at the start of Genesis, a work then seen as pregnant with concealed and vital meaning, made it an apt subject for speculative exploration. The words 'In the beginning' in Gen. i. 1 could be read instrumentally, to say that God created 'by means of' this mysterious 'beginning'. But according

[1] Not always so: elsewhere 'we' joins writer and recipients as the true believers (e.g. i. 6), and, elsewhere again, serves to distinguish them from the heretics (e.g. iii. 19). See K. Weiss, 'Orthodoxie und Heterodoxie in 1. Johannesbrief', *ZNW*, 58, 1967, pp. 247 ff.

to other texts, e.g. Ps. xxxiii. 6; Wis. ix. 1, it was by his word or his wisdom that God performed his creative work. So **the beginning** could be read as a term for the creative agent of God, and it may be that speculation along these lines lies behind Col. i. 15-20 (cf. W. D. Davies, *Paul and Rabbinic Judaism*, London, 1948, pp. 150 ff.). But even without this flight of speculation, **the beginning** could still be used in an absolute sense—for the very roots of all time and space. In this sense it occurs in GJ i. 1, and elsewhere in the Gospel. Indeed almost every occurrence may bear this sense (i. 2; vi. 64; viii. 44). But here, almost certainly, it is different. It refers to the origins of the Christian preaching—**the word of life**. That was the time on which the writer takes his stand, the time from which the authentic faith stems and by which alone it is to be tested. Other occurrences of the word bear this out: ii. 7, 24; iii. 11; 2J 5 f.; but not 1J ii. 13 f. or iii. 8 where it is used in the deeper sense. There is no question here of the preexistence of Christ, which leads to the absolute use of the term in GJ i. 1: attention focuses rather on the moment of his appearance in the flesh, the great fact on which our writer insists. Once more we observe not only the doctrinal emphases of the writer, no doubt intensified by the needs of controversy, but also the relative simplicity and unspeculative quality of his mind.

The writer of these verses felt constrained to echo the opening of GJ, though his concerns and emphases were different. Why did he feel this constraint? Why did he not write freely and why did he think it desirable to establish a connection at the start, so deliberately? Once more, other early Christian writings come up for comparison. The question arises whether the Epistle is not one among a number of works which leaned upon the authority of a previous composition and hoped to flourish under its aegis. In a case like that of Ephesians in relation to Colossians, open pseudonymity is used: the writer takes the name of Paul, as a cloak to lend dignity and force to his own work (cf. J. L. Houlden, *Paul's Letters from Prison*, Harmondsworth, 1970, p. 240). In our present case, no name is at stake (that was only to be supplied later, cf. pp. 38 ff.); except possibly, covertly, that of the Beloved Disciple, for it may be that the appendix to GJ is not unconnected with 1J (GJ xxi. 24). But the principle may well be identical. The congregation from which these writings come is both pushing its work one stage further and, under the pressure of controversy and schism, looking back anxiously to its foundations (cf. p. 14). With what justice this writer, as against his opponents, claimed the mantle of GJ, is a matter on which there were already at the time of writing no doubt two opinions.

Bultmann (*Exegetica*, p. 381) can speak of these verses as 'formed with literary art'. The grammatical roughness, which on any showing renders the precise meaning obscure, need not necessarily invalidate that judgement. The passage has grandeur. It is a proclamation of the message by which the writer stands against all comers, and the essence of it is clear: the vital importance of the historical origins of God's act in Christ, whereby the Christians' fellowship has been established. The rest of the Epistle does little more than develop it.

We turn now to the flow of ideas and the detailed wording. The words come in bursts, and the first task is to decide where the breaks should be placed. In *v*. 1 should there be a pause before **concerning the word of life**, so that this phrase defines the area with which what **we** have heard, seen and felt is concerned—it is all connected with the word of life? Or should there be no pause, so that the phrase states the theme, in relation to which information is included under the four clauses beginning **that which**? The distinction is perhaps not very great—it is a matter of the strength of attachment between the clauses and the phrase. But the former way of taking it is better, because though the phrase flows well from the last three clauses, the first of the four must stand on its own, and as all four are parallel, it is better to treat all alike and provide a pause.

Another question has some bearing upon the matter: the meaning of **the word of life**. In the Gospel prologue, 'Word' (*logos*) is a title, almost a name, for Jesus, preexistent, then incarnate. The ascription of this term to a person was an understandable development, on the basis of both Jewish usage and contemporary Hellenistic philosophy. Jewish speculation, seen in the prophets, psalms and wisdom writing, had already in varying degrees personified the notion of the powerful and active word of God, and such speculation had deep roots in the thought of other peoples of the ancient world, Egypt in particular (cf. S. G. F. Brandon in ed. F. F. Bruce and E. G. Rupp, *Holy Book and Holy Tradition*, Manchester, 1968). The main Old Testament references are Is. lv. 10 f.; Ps. xxxiii. 6; Wis. ix. 1; xviii. 15. Aided by the Stoic use of the term, to signify the rational principle inherent in and giving unity to all things, Philo, the Jewish writer of Alexandria in the earlier half of the first century after Christ, had given new currency to this strand in biblical imagery. It is then not surprising that, just as Paul uses the closely parallel idea of God's wisdom as a way of giving expression to his conviction of Christ's universal significance, so another part of the Christian body worked with the concept of the word.

However, in GJ the idea is not carried beyond the prologue, and there are many uses of the term in the much more common Old Testament sense of the message of God or of Jesus, e.g. v. 24, 28; viii. 31; xiv. 23; xv. 3. So the question arises: despite the Gospel prologue, how deeply embedded in the Johannine circle was the strong, personal sense of 'the word' (*logos*) applied to Jesus? Was it so firm that it must bear this sense in 1J i. 1-4— which, as we have seen, depends in general upon the opening of the Gospel? Yet will its use here bear this interpretation? If we take the phrase in isolation, the answer is No. The natural sense is 'the message that gives life'. And Johannine parallels (to go no further) like 'bread of life' (GJ vi. 35), 'resurrection of life' (GJ v. 29), and indeed 'words (*rhēmata* not *logoi*) of life' (GJ vi. 68) tell in its favour. (For the phrase itself there is a Pauline parallel, Phil. ii. 16.) On the other hand, if the connection with the verbs **have seen, felt**, is to be at all close, then it is hard to see how this can be the right sense: the reference must be to a person. But if **word** here refers to Jesus, it is strange to find the addition of the words **of life**. If the term was to be added at all, we might have expected the form 'and the life' (cf. GJ xi. 25; xiv. 6). And it is surprising that the writer did not in that case prefer to use the masculine 'he whom' rather than the neuter **that which** in the four clauses, and then omit **concerning**. These verses would then have been a development of GJ i. 14, with an opening reminiscence of GJ i. 1 (with **beginning** in its absolute sense). On any showing, can **that which our hands felt** have any other than a personal reference, and can the neuter pronoun, in this case at least, be other than inappropriate?

The upshot seems to be that if we place no break before **concerning the word of life**, 'word' may but need not signify Jesus—the writer is listing the numerous links with him. If we do place a break at that point, then it is more likely to mean 'message', and the four clauses and the phrase are simply two ways of referring to the same thing, that is 'the Christian proclamation'—the former by way of content, the latter by way of theme (cf. C. H. Dodd, Commentary, p. 3). In neither case has the writer made his meaning crystal clear, and the ambiguity may even be deliberate. Jesus gave the word and embodied it. But it is hard to resist the view that either his understanding of the Gospel prologue is defective or he deliberately opts for a less speculative theology and yet chooses to express those beliefs which were crucial to him in terms already venerable in Johannine ears.

*V.* 2 does a little to clear up the ambiguity. Though **life** can stand for Jesus (cf. GJ xi. 25; xiv. 6)—*Jesus* was revealed—there is no parallel to the use of **eternal life** (*v.* 2*b*) in this way; and the use of this term after **we saw** (one of the verbs in *v.* 1) perhaps tips the balance in favour of the dominant reference in *v.* 1 being to the Christian message rather than to Jesus. Once more the theology is lightened and the speculative tone muted by comparison with the Gospel: whereas in GJ i. 1, it was the Word who was 'with God' and then revealed, here the same expression is used of **eternal life** (**with** = *pros*).

At first reading, and traditionally, this passage has always been taken as clear evidence that the Epistle is the work of an eyewitness of Jesus' life. Whether **word** refers to him or to the Gospel message, though more clearly in the former case, this is the most natural inference. In common with most modern critics, we take it that this is not so. As we have shown (cf. Introduction, pp. 1 ff.), the concerns of this writer all point to a date when eyewitnesses can hardly have been plentiful. The later association with John the Apostle was an attempt to give body to such a figure, but there is no reason to believe that to be a genuine tradition (cf. pp. 38 ff.). But if **we** does not refer to an eyewitness, to whom does it refer? It expresses, we have said (p. 48), authoritative Christian opinion. But what position is the authoritative figure attempting to occupy? When he affirms that **we** saw, heard and felt, is he claiming solidarity with all true Christians, from the start; or, bluntly, is he, in writing as if he were an eyewitness, deliberately setting out to deceive, in order to further his cause? This would not be impossible: pseudonymous writing could easily merge into what we should call forgery (cf. K. Aland, *JTS*, 12, 1961); and in a period when the search for authorities was becoming urgent among the

Christian congregations, recourse to this expedient soon became common. But in this case it is unlikely, for both the writer's audience and those whom he attacks seem to be close to him. It is more probable that he consciously takes the mantle of orthodoxy: he speaks for and is at one with all those who have thought rightly about Jesus **from the beginning**—and of course that includes those who first saw, heard and felt. He identifies himself with them, as Jews had long been able to identify themselves with the great deeds of their ancestors (cf. Deut. xxix. 5 f.).

It is possible that there is another element, and the closer our writer is to the mind behind GJ, the more likely it is to be present. It lies in the reference to **that which we have seen with our own eyes**. Is it necessary, as appears at first sight, that this indicates, in whatever sense, an eyewitness of Jesus' life? The image of seeing was, as it has often been, a commonplace for religious faith or insight, and GJ makes considerable play with it. The story of the man born blind (ch. ix) turns upon it, and in xii. 40, a well-known passage is quoted from Isaiah which uses the same idea. To see with the eyes is to have faith; to have blind eyes is to lack faith. In xx. 24, by contrast, a distinction is drawn between sight and faith: attention is directed to those who believe without having seen and they are accounted blessed. Nevertheless, in our passage it may well be that the ambiguity of the expression is a positive aid. It helps to bind the writer to those who stand behind him, those who literally saw Jesus and witnessed the original events of the life-giving Gospel. Whatever force there is in this must not diminish in the slightest the emphasis on the historical occurrence, which is vital to the writer's polemic against those who do not believe that the saviour came fully **in the flesh** (iv. 2). The idea of hearing (*v.* 1) can bear similar treatment, though nowhere does GJ make use of it in this way.

The touching of Jesus appears twice in GJ, in both cases in connection with his resurrection body. Mary Magdalene in the garden is told not to touch (or perhaps to cease touching), xx. 17, and Thomas, having asserted that only touching would convince him, is invited to do so when Jesus appears, xx. 24. For the writer of GJ, as for the writer of 1J, touching is somehow closely linked with awareness of the risen Christ. Is it the case that, however obscurely the matter is put, touching like seeing is meant to be a way of expressing identity with the earlier believers, perhaps not so much with those who knew the Jesus of the time before his death as those who have believed in his risen power?

As we have seen in the course of our exposition, most of the vocabulary of these verses is also found in GJ, though this is not true of **fellowship** (*koinōnia*). But the word reappears in the first main section of 1J, in i. 6 f., and accords well with the Johannine concern for unity in the Christian body.

For **our joy** a number of manuscripts read 'your joy'. This variant is common throughout the work, as in other Greek writings. It arises because the words differ only by a vowel. The two vowels were pronounced alike and easily mistaken when the copying of manuscripts was carried out by dictation. The passage will bear either sense.

It will be noticed that there is nothing in these verses to justify the title 'Epistle': we may contrast the openings of 2J and 3J. Though this writing is clearly addressed to a church, and so far merits the traditional classification, it lacks the formal marks of a letter, and is best regarded as a hortatory treatise, directed to an intimately known audience. The nature of the work becomes clearer once its structure is determined, cf. pp. 22 ff.

## 2. THE TWO WAYS
### i. 5–ii. 11

**(5) And the message which we heard from him and are announcing to you is this: God is light and there is no darkness whatsoever in him. (6) If we say that we have fellowship with him yet walk in the darkness, we are liars and are not acting according to the truth. (7) But if we walk in the light, as he is in the light, then we have fellowship with each other and the blood of Jesus his Son cleanses us from all sin. (8) If we say that we have no sin, we deceive ourselves and there is no truth in us. (9) If we confess our sins, he is faithful and righteous—which means that he will forgive our sins and purify us from all sin. (10) If we say that we have not sinned, we make him a liar, and his word is not in us. (ii. 1) My children, I am writing this to you so that you may not sin. But if anyone does sin, we have someone to speak on our**

behalf to the Father, that is Jesus Christ, the righteous one.
(2) And he is a sacrificial offering for our sins—and not only
for ours, but for those of the whole world. (3) And this is how
we know that we have come to know him—if we keep his
commands. (4) The man who says, I know him, and fails to
keep his commands, is a liar and the truth is not in him.
(5) But as for the man who keeps his word, God's love is
perfected in him. This is how we know that we exist in him:
(6) anyone who says that he dwells in him ought so to walk
as he walked.

(7) My dear ones, I have no new command to write to you,
but an old command—one that you have had from the
beginning. This old command is the message which you
heard. (8) But again, in a sense, I do write you a new command—something true in relation to both him and you—
because the darkness is passing away and the true light is
already shining. (9) The man who says he is in the light and
hates his brother is still very much in the darkness. (10) The
man who loves his brother dwells in the light and there is
nothing to make him stumble; (11) but the man who hates
his brother exists in the darkness and walks in the darkness
—he does not know where he is going because the darkness
has made him blind.

This passage, the first main section of the work, brings to the
fore straightaway one of its main concerns: the question of sin in
the life of the Christian. Why does it exist? How is it to be dealt
with? As we shall see, the writer's teaching is not wholly clear. It
is in fact so inconsistent (and iii. 9 sharpens the inconsistency) that
scholars have often come to the belief that the work stems from
more than one hand or was written by stages. So it may be; but
if we bear in mind one underlying conviction we shall be better
placed to understand why obscurity was likely to arise in relation
to this matter. The conviction is that on becoming a Christian a
man is transferred from the realm of sin or darkness to the realm
of righteousness, truth or light. Because he sees these as two
distinct realities, any evidence that the transfer is imperfect or
incomplete is hard for our writer to assimilate. Yet the evidence
is before his eyes: Christians sin, and as their pastor he must offer
both a rationale and a remedy.

His position is made harder by the fact that some Christians find an easy way out of the difficulty. Flying in the face of the moral facts and remembering only the new status they have received, they assert that Christians cannot and do not sin. And, presumably, acts which would be sinful when committed by others, simply do not bear this character when done by them.

For our writer, this solution is not possible. His hold on moral realities is too strong. His metaphysical picture is not so strong that it breaks his moral picture. Neither, however, is the contrary true. He does not abandon the teaching which he has received (cf. GJ v. 24), which distinguishes sharply between the sphere of existence from which the believer comes and that into which he is brought. The two pictures are hard to fit together, and inconsistency is inevitable. It is seen at its sharpest if we compare i. 8 and iii. 9: on the one hand, to claim sinlessness is sheer self-deception, on the other, the child of God is incapable of sin. It is possible to mitigate the problem. The sense of i. 7 may be that the sacrifice of Jesus serves to obliterate a Christian's sins as soon as they are done, so that substantially his walking in the light is undisturbed. And this is accompanied by the assurance of Jesus' advocacy at the Father's court (ii. 1). Or we may look ahead to the pastoral casuistry of v. 16 f. and suppose it is in mind in our present passage: what is in question here is the trivial sin. Such offences can be dealt with without any spoiling of the Christian's status as one who shares fellowship with God and walks in the light. With serious sin, it would be different and nothing that is said here about forgiveness applies to that.

Or else we may speak of variety of emphasis. The writer adopts first one standpoint and then another, and neither is adopted so fixedly as to make the other a confusing element. Neither is to be taken too far: it would be as false to see Christian life as conferring magical immunity from sin as to suppose that continual sinfulness is accepted as a matter of routine. But this evades the issue. Our writer is, in a sense, the victim of his world-outlook. It simply does not allow him to incorporate into a single frame all that he is bound to say. This is true whether he is composing freely or whether he is using accepted formulae and commenting on them in the light of problems now freshly posed. In either case, we may take it that he is ready to stand by what he writes. It represents what he believes, and in that there is an irreducible duality.

The theological core of his world-picture comes at the start: **God is light and there is no darkness whatsoever in him**. It is stated deliberately, firmly and solemnly. But the moral implications are given immediately. Accepting the doctrine entails appropriate conduct. We shall find this to be a constant feature of 1J.

The doctrinal formulation in *v.* 5 is clearly fundamental. But in the context of the religious thought of the time it is quite unremarkable. The division of reality into two spheres, seen as light and darkness, is commonplace. It is found for example in Jewish sources from a few decades earlier. In the Community Rule of Qumran (1QS iii) we read words strongly reminiscent of our present passage: ' Those born of truth spring from a fountain of light, but those born of falsehood spring from a source of darkness. All the children of righteousness are ruled by the Prince of Light and walk in the ways of light; but all the children of falsehood are ruled by the Angel of Darkness and walk in the ways of darkness' (Vermes, pp. 75 f.). (Cf. also Charlesworth, op. cit., pp. 156 ff.) It would be hard to think of a closer parallel. But the distinction itself is thoroughly familiar also in Hellenistic religion (cf. C. H. Dodd, *The Interpretation of the Fourth Gospel*, Cambridge, 1953, pp. 10, 18, 34–6, 201 ff.). And Philo, the Hellenistic Jew of the first century, looking back to Ps. xxvii. 1 ('The Lord is my light'), actually duplicates our present passage. 'God is light', he wrote (*De Somniis*, i. 75), but then, with greater philosophical refinement, in the Platonist manner, he adds, safeguarding the divine transcendence, 'and not light only, but the archetype of every other light; or rather, more ancient and higher than any archetype.' It was an important element in the agreed basis of thought which was shared by the orthodox Christian thinkers and many of the heretics of the second century, and it is hard to believe that any opponents whom our writer is likely to be facing would have found any difficulty in accepting this proposition.

Indeed, precisely this fact was probably an embarrassment to him, and explains why he hastens to expound it in his own terms. For it could bear other interpretations, and his own was in some ways not the most clear-cut, as we have seen; nor was it, in the eyes of many, the most attractive.

The many people of the Eastern Mediterranean world of the late first century who turned their minds towards serious reflection on the universe found it on the whole a disturbing and daunting place. It was full of uncertainties, hazards and calamities which gave no hope of recovery. It was inevitable that men should despair of such a world and then seek to escape its threats. In the obvious, practical sense, such escape was impossible—sooner or later, disaster, whether in the shape of natural occurrence, sickness or death, would overtake everyone, and always it hung over everyone, menacingly. Any escape route could only be in the realm of the spiritual or in a life after death. The more appalled people were by the intractability of life's circumstances, the sharper the division they were likely to make between the world of experience and the 'other world'. The sharpest possible way of making the division was to associate God (and all desirable things) exclusively with the latter and give him no part whatsoever in the existence or affairs of the former. God, the repository of all that was attractive, on whom hope was pinned, could have had no share in the creation of the world. It had resulted from some catastrophic error: the myth-making instinct did not fail to clothe the theory with story (cf. Jonas, op. cit., pp. 112 ff.).

The statement in *v.* 5 is a perfect brief expression of such belief —provided that **darkness** signifies the whole of experienced reality. The world was the realm of darkness; by definition it was the very antithesis of God. Man's only hope lay in finding a way of extracting himself from it—or being extracted, by a saviour from the divine side—and attaching himself to God.

Such was the most absolute way of understanding the duality in human experience—the duality of happiness and misery, hope kindled then dashed, life on the way to fulfilment then frustrated and crushed: especially when the negative aspect seemed always to be uppermost.

But such a judgement, attractive just by reason of its simplicity and absoluteness, failed to take account of the complexity and subtlety of experience—and of certain powerful elements in the traditional understanding of God and the world, especially as far as Judaism was concerned. In particular, by breaking the link between God and the world, abandoning effectively his ultimate responsibility for it and power over it as creator, it cast off an age-old conviction. For many whose background and formation lay in Judaism (such as the men of Qumran who, as we have seen, still accepted much of this picture) that step was impossible.

It also failed to do justice to the moral sense. It might be under-

standable to react to the diverse character of human life by feeling
the happiness to be negligible by comparison with the misery, and
hope of bliss to be possible only in the future. But once a man
turned his attention to the moral aspect of experience, it was not
so easy to see moral aspiration as an empty gesture, devoid of
meaning. For such a man, the cleavage between light and darkness
here and now might seem neither so clear nor so absolute. Secure
salvation might lie beyond but now in this life the moral struggle
was genuine and serious—and God was involved in it. Human
thought and action were not to be abandoned as of no concern to
God, part and parcel of the realm of darkness, but were themselves
the area within which the moral battle was fought. Light and
darkness were inextricably mixed in the very heart of man and in
the conduct which sprang from it. **God is light and there is no
darkness whatsoever in him**: but this does not mean that he is
not involved in human life, or that the sphere of morality is outside his concern. Quite the contrary, the moral struggle is to be
accepted and engaged in by those who attach themselves to him.

That, whatever the apparent inconsistency, this is the underlying pattern of thought in this passage, becomes clear from *v.* 8
onwards. The dualism of the cosmos is modified by the moral
realities of human life. In another respect too the conception of
reality as divided between light and darkness is rendered less
absolute than it appears at first sight—and less absolute than it
would have been in much non-Jewish religious speculation. The
darkness is not ranged permanently against the light, it is already
**passing away** (ii. 8). Once more, this writer shares the Jewish
perspective according to which God will act to vindicate his cosmic
rule; and, beyond that, he shares the Christian perspective whereby that action has begun in the coming of Christ: **the true light
is already shining**.

We have considered the key pronouncement in *v.* 5 in the light
of the wider background and in the context of this writer's thought.
If we look at it in relation to the Johannine Gospel, we shall be
struck by the fact that it concerns God, not Christ. In GJ viii. 12
and ix. 5, Jesus refers to himself as 'the light of the world' and in
GJ i. 4, 9 he is described in terms of light. The difference between
the two writings in this matter is typical. Though Christ is as
vital in 1J as in any early Christian writing, doctrinal statement
concerning him is much less developed than in GJ. There, a

series of high titles and attributes, full of doctrinal significance, is applied to him, their effect being to depict him as the unique mediator of God to man. Here the range of titles is much more restricted and much less adventurous. He is the Messiah (ii. 22), the Son (i. 3; iii. 23), the sacrificial offering (i. 7; ii. 2; iv. 10), and the advocate or spokesman (ii. 1). But the more abstract titles are reserved for God: here, 'light', and, in iv. 8 and 16, 'love' (in GJ, compare only, 'God is spirit', iv. 24).[1] In this sense, the Epistle is more theocentric and less christocentric in its theological standpoint than the Gospel. Or, to put it another way, the Gospel's christology is much more developed than that of the Epistle. It is true that the expression **the true light** (ii. 8) may refer to Jesus, and if it occurred in GJ would almost certainly do so. But here we cannot be so sure. In the light of the firm statement of i. 5 it may be that, like **word** in i. 4, **light** has here a more general reference. **The true light** is not so much Christ himself as the fact of his coming or the Gospel message.

This may throw light on another question raised by these verses: their connection with the preceding section. In *v.* 5, the object of hearing and announcing is **the message**. Does this not confirm that, whatever element of reference to Jesus there may also be, the main content of **that which we heard** (*v.* 1) is doctrine and that **the word of life** defines the effect and purpose of the teaching which is now crystallized in the statement in *v.* 5?

But how can a theological proposition be identified with what has been seen, heard and touched? In other words, how is the emphasis on historical, factual origins connected with an abstract tenet such as **God is light**? The writer does nothing to show his logic clearly; but he sees the message of Jesus, guaranteed by the witness of men's senses, as the truth that **God is light**, a statement found nowhere in the tradition of Jesus' teaching known to us, whether in GJ or elsewhere. It is impossible to say whether the writer believed it to be a saying of Jesus or gives it as the epitome of his teaching.

This message is life-giving (*v.* 2): to accept it is to receive salvation. The following verses show how this is so. The proposition is no mere abstract truth. It is the basis for walking in the

[1] Bultmann, *Commentary*, p. 21, points out that these statements are not to be taken as giving 'a definition of God's being, how God is in himself. (They) signify rather what God means for man.'

right path, in practical terms for right conduct. The later insistence that Jesus came in the flesh (iv. 2) may well illuminate the connections of thought which are only just discernible in this passage. For this writer, Jesus' historical reality and perhaps the moral demand present in his teaching are the basis for a doctrine of God which retains seriousness about ethics while speaking dualist language—a union which others failed to maintain.

Human realities assert themselves. It is one thing to quit the realm of darkness and enter the sphere of light—and to recognize its moral implications. It is another to succeed in living the moral life. How is the gap between aspiration and success to be bridged? At this point, and without any sign of incongruity, the writer calls upon a concept which belongs originally to a quite different sphere of discourse from that of the abstract, almost philosophical, religious categories in which the argument has so far been couched. He appeals to the world of ritual sacrifice, equally part of his Jewish-based religious culture.

The reasoning seems to be this. As a Christian, he is aware not only of the gap between what is demanded in the moral sphere and what is achieved. He is aware too that God does not hold his people's failure (at least in all cases, cf. v. 16 f.) against them. The discrepancy is not necessarily a ground for despair. On the contrary, they are to continue to tread the Christian path. This at first sight impossible combination of elements is somehow reconciled—and Jesus is at the heart of the reconciliation. In this world of thought, Jewish at root, to experience reconciliation is to know the fruit of sacrifice, for sacrifice is the means by which sin is removed. Jesus, then, fulfils the role of a sacrificial offering in shedding his blood in death (i. 7), indeed *is* such an offering (*hilasmos*, ii. 2). He removes sins. Cf. also v. 6 and GJ xix. 34; p. 127.

The word is of the same family as that used by Paul, Rom. iii. 25 (cf. also 1 Peter i. 18 f.). It is nowhere used in GJ, though i. 29 and 36 show the idea is not alien to that work, and critics inclined to underplay the Jewish background of 1J, or to judge the Epistle by the Gospel, see in both i. 7*b* and ii. 2 the infiltration of a piece of 'ordinary' church jargon. Especially in the former case, where a pattern of more abstract statements in parallelism is disturbed, formal literary considerations may be taken to confirm this judgement (cf. p. 28). But the more the Jewish quality of the thought of 1J is recognized, the more the collocation of ideas, disparate in

origin indeed, but all at home already in Judaism, need occasion
no surprise.

*Hilasmos*, which we have translated by the general term 'sacrificial offering', may well carry the more specific idea of 'propitia-
tion', and its association with the term *paraklētos* ('advocate',
below, p. 64) in *v.* 1 confirms the presence of that idea here.
Both images carry the idea of winning over the party to whom
appeal is made or sacrifice offered. But there is no element of
anxiety in this 'winning over'. On the contrary, God is **faithful
and righteous** (i. 9), and he is at one with the action of **the blood
of Jesus his Son** in cleansing us from sin (i. 7 and 9). (For *hilasmos*,
see D. Hill, *Greek Words and Hebrew Meanings*, Cambridge, 1967,
pp. 36 ff.)

Forgiveness is available, but obedience to God's command is
still the test of allegiance. The command is simple: to love one's
Christian brothers. Time and again in this writing, but first in
ii. 9–11, the writer insists on the absolute necessity of brotherly
love, as the one clear test of the sphere to which a man belongs.
No evasion is tolerated (ii. 4). Nothing can be a substitute for it
and nothing is needed in addition to it. Yet it is not a self-contained
objective, for it brings with it a full share of God's love (ii. 5).

In the light of the numerous references to the duty to love being
directed towards **each other** (iii. 11, 23; iv. 7, 11, 12; cf. 2J 5), and
of the fact that the command to love in GJ is expressed in the
same terms (xiii. 34; xv. 12, 17), there can be no serious doubt that
the **brother** in ii. 9 and 10 means the fellow-Christian—as clearly
in iii. 13 (cf. also iii. 15; iv. 20).[1] The writer's moral as well as
doctrinal horizon is set at the Christian congregation which he
believes to be laden with a cosmic destiny. It alone has received
the true and saving message. It is our writer's practical belief that
salvation is confined to those who walk in the light. Only two
possibilities are envisaged (ii. 9, 10), and a man takes one or the
other; though self-deception (are the heretics in mind, *v.* 9?) is
easy. We find the same quality of community-consciousness at
Qumran: it is required of the brethren that 'they may love all the
sons of light, each according to his lot in God's design, and hate
all the sons of darkness, each according to his guilt in God's
vengeance' (Vermes, p. 72). It comes then as something of a

---

[1] Bultmann, Commentary, p. 35, asserts, without argument, that it has the
wider meaning of 'neighbour'.

surprise when we read that Christ is the offering not only for the sins of the Christians, but **for those of the whole world** (ii. 2; cf. iv. 14). Is this a piece of unthought-out rhetoric, or is there some way in which we can regard it as of a piece with the rest of the writer's thought about the world, of which iv. 9 f., with its idea of the saving emissary who comes into the world for the sake of the few, seems a much more characteristic expression? It does not stand alone in the Johannine writings. Christ is seen as the one who removes the sins of the world in GJ i. 29; and in GJ xii. 32, his being lifted up on the Cross will draw all men to himself. Similarly, his coming was for the salvation of 'the world' (GJ iii. 17). It is doubtful whether the writer would have been able to give a thoroughly satisfactory account which reconciled these universalist and positive statements with his predominantly 'anti-world' outlook[1] (cf. ii. 15; v. 19) and his strong sense of the inner community of the elect within which the duty of love, so much more widely expressed in the synoptic Gospels (cf. Mark xii. 31; Matt. v. 44; Luke x. 25-37), is confined. Certainly he nowhere even hints at an explanation—as if he were unaware of any difficulty.

It is unlikely that the solution is to be sought along the lines of unfulfilled or impracticable aspiration. More probably, it is to be found in terms of eschatology, and as a consequence of the writer's sense of God as the creator. This belief, it is true, is not expressed in 1J, but it appears in GJ i. 1-3 and we can be sure that our writer, despite his pessimism about the world, would not have denied it. If God's creative power is cosmic in scope, so, in some way, will be his power to consummate all things—whatever the conflict of light and darkness in the meantime. For, in Jewish belief, the End would, in numerous ways, correspond to the Beginning, and the ultimately unchallengeable nature of God's power had to be

[1] More of the references to the world are negative in tone in 1J than in GJ (in fact all except ii. 2 and iv. 14, possibly together with iv. 9 and 17). Perhaps 1J is too short for this to be significant. But if it is, then it is surprising, in the light of a general thesis that 1J represents, in relation to GJ, a Johannine withdrawal from 'Gnostic' positions by contrast with those who have advanced further in that direction. But we have observed (p. 15) considerable confusion in the mind of our writer; and though he has two clearly doctrinal 'anti-world' statements of great rigour (ii. 15 and v. 19), much of his attitude in this regard may be attributable to his increased concern with the Church's inner affairs, as against the Gospel's concentration on the wider issues of revelation and redemption (cf. N. H. Cassem, *NTS*, 19, 1972, pp. 81 ff.).

affirmed. So the universalist affirmations must be made, however incongruous they may seem to us when placed alongside other ideas.

Christ is described not only as a sacrificial offering, but also as **someone to speak on our behalf to the Father**—our advocate and spokesman. The image is that of the royal court at which a suppliant needs someone greater than himself, who has the ear of the king, to plead his cause. Jesus performs this role with the Father on behalf of the Christians. The term is *paraklētos*—our translation is a periphrasis, for want of a wholly suitable single word. It is used in GJ for the Spirit which is to succeed to Jesus' position as defender and strengthener of the disciples after his death (xiv. 16 f., 26; xv. 26; xvi. 7). But in GJ, Jesus himself is, if not *the*, then certainly a *paraklētos*, for in xiv. 16, the Spirit is '*another* comforter'.[1] In 1J however, the role is different. Jesus is now not the disciples' defender in face of the world or the strengthener of their common life, but their spokesman in relation to the Father.

He performs his role by virtue of his being **righteous** (*dikaios*), that is, sinless. Here the link is made with the reference to sacrifice in i. 7 and ii. 2. An effective offering must be spotless, without blemish. So too Jesus as the leader of God's people must be blameless. This idea again is Jewish. Great efforts were made to keep the priests of Israel in a state of ceremonial purity before they performed their tasks (cf. J. Jeremias, *Jerusalem in the Time of Jesus*, London, 1969, pp. 152–4), and at Qumran the same concept appears, with the poor, righteous man as the spokesman in the community's psalms and the teacher of righteousness as the revered leader (cf. Charlesworth, op. cit., pp. 25–30). Jesus, now exalted to heaven, after carrying out the sacrificial task, can speak the more effectively to the Father on his followers' behalf: his sinlessness matches that of God himself and enables him to approach him (cf. the use of *dikaios* to describe God in i. 9).

But if Jesus occupies this role of intercessor on behalf of his followers, the condition that he will be heard is that they confess their sins—formally, we may suppose, before the congregation (i. 9).

---

[1] For this word and its two leading senses, 'advocate' and 'comforter', the former *vis à vis* an outsider, whether, as here, God, or, in GJ, the world, the latter *vis à vis* the Christian community itself, see C. K. Barrett, *The Gospel According to St John*, London, 1955, pp. 385 f.

In the provision of this procedure, the Johannine community is once again similar to Qumran: 'All those entering the Covenant shall confess and say: We have strayed. We have disobeyed. We and our fathers before us have sinned....And the Priests shall bless all the men of the lot of God who walk perfectly in all his ways, saying: May he bless you with all good and preserve you from all evil. May he lighten your heart with life-giving wisdom and grant you eternal knowledge. May he raise his merciful face towards you for everlasting bliss' (Vermes, p. 73). Dealing with the sins of the believers is not merely a theoretical matter: it is practical, and there is a way to tackle it (cf. also v. 16 f.).

In ii. 3, we have the first of many (twenty-five in all) uses of the verb 'to know' (*ginōskō*), and of a characteristic construction with that verb: literally, 'by this we know that...' (used nine times, with minor variations, cf. p. 31). In the preceding verses, looking back to i. 3, the believers' link with God has been expressed in terms of **fellowship** (*koinōnia*). Now, and in much of the rest of the Epistle, 'knowledge' comes to the forefront. To be a Christian is to have knowledge—in a wide variety of ways. Here it is knowledge about coming to know God.

'Knowledge' (*gnōsis*) was one of the great objects of religious aspiration in this period, so much so that this aspect of religious feeling gave its name to a whole movement of piety and theology—Gnosticism (cf. p. 9 n.). Already, in the first century, the roots of that movement are to be seen in both Hellenistic and Jewish religion (see the quotation above from the Community Rule from Qumran). Our writer shares many of its assumptions and tendencies. Nevertheless, the noun, *gnōsis*, occurs neither here nor in GJ, though the verb is common in both. In early Christian writings, the noun appears most frequently in Paul, sometimes with a sense close to that with which we are here concerned and sometimes by way of controverting opponents who appear to lay great store by it (1 Cor. i. 5; viii. 1, 10; xiii. 12; xiv. 6; Rom. ii. 20). It has often been suggested that because of its doubtful connections, the Johannine writers deliberately avoided the word, but this is scarcely convincing when they use the verb so freely and when they show themselves so willing to express ideas which are Gnostic in tendency. In any case, we have no reason to suppose that the word 'knowledge' in itself was one which would arouse so sensitive a reaction at this date.

The writer of 1J is much concerned with the bases of faith—
this is the explanation of his frequent use of 'know' and the catch-
phrase in which it occurs. He seeks time and again to arrive at the
essential content of the message by which he stands—**the word of
life** (i. 1)—and to explore the routes by which it may be known for
sure. Here, as we should expect, he makes immediately the connection with ethics: How do we know that we have come to know
him? **If we keep his commands** (ii. 4; cf. also ii. 6). Knowledge
of God is not speculative and abstract, but practical and experiential. And in each of these tests, we shall not be wrong if we see
a reference to the heretics and their failure to measure up to what
is required.

One other word needs to be brought into prominence: **truth**
(*alētheia*). To a degree, its sense is expressed in the formula: as
the 'light–darkness' antithesis is in giving an account of reality,
so is the 'truth–sin' antithesis in the area of morals. The correspondence is not perfect in that 'righteousness' also occurs as the
opposite of 'sin', and 'truth' carries in part an ontological reference. It overlaps with 'light' in describing the sphere of God's rule
into which the believer is brought and in which he dwells. Nevertheless, it is not a deeply philosophical or abstract word, either
here or, probably, in GJ. The expression translated **acting
according to the truth** means something like 'behaving with
integrity' (i. 6). It is, literally, 'doing the truth', and occurs also
in GJ iii. 21; it shows clearly the word's practical and ethical
bearing. **Truth** is genuineness and soundness. The background
is firmly Jewish. In this sense, God's conduct can be spoken of as
characterized by 'truth', cf. Ex. xxxiv. 6, and the DSS have the
very phrase—the members of the community of Qumran, like
those of the Johannine congregation, are to 'do the truth' (1QS i.
5; v. 3; viii. 2; especially Vermes, p. 78). (On 'truth' in Johannine
usage, see S. Aalen, *Studia Evangelica*, ii, Berlin, 1964, pp. 3–24.)

The more obvious opposite of truth—falsehood—also occurs:
in i. 6 and ii. 4 the two words are placed closely together. To lie
is however not (except partly in iv. 20) to tell untruth: it is to act
dishonestly—to go against the demands of integrity; and in v. 10,
failure to trust God is seen as tantamount to accusing him of such
dishonesty.

'To walk' in the sense of 'to live and act' (i. 6 f.; ii. 6, 11) causes
no difficulty, but the word's associations are worth noting. The

Torah (the Law) means 'the way', and frequently in Judaism life is seen as a path given by God, or a journey to be undertaken in God's company. The piety expressed in Ps. cxix makes great use of the image: the word 'way' occurs no less than nineteen times. Teaching concerning the two ways of life—the way of goodness and life and the way of evil and death—was standard in Judaism (Deut. xxx. 15; 1QS iii. 13–iv. 26, Vermes, pp. 75 ff.; cf. the Christian use in Didache i, *ECW*, p. 227). The word used here, *peripateō*, is not common in this sense in the LXX, but in Prov. viii. 20 we find, 'I walk in the paths of righteousness' (cf. also Eccles. xi. 9). In the NT, however, it occurs frequently, especially in Paul and in GJ: Rom. vi. 4; Gal. v. 25; GJ viii. 12; xi. 7 f.; xii. 35. In GJ xiv. 6, the idea is exploited, characteristically, for the purposes of christology: Jesus, superseding the Torah, is 'the way'.

Not only the content but the literary form of these verses is reminiscent of Jewish writing. Both the carefully antithetical statements (i. 6–10) and the more hortatory passages have their parallels (cf. p. 29).

There remains one important point of interpretation. What are we to make of the play on the newness and/or oldness of the command in ii. 7? It is one of the clearest indications that the Epistle is later than and presupposes the Johannine Gospel. There, the command to love one another is referred to as 'new' (xiii. 34). Now however it is 'old', for it has been continuous in the Christian brotherhood **from the beginning** (*v.* 7), and this age and continuity is something on which our writer insists. It is the source of authority for the command, which is a central point of his argument. Yet it remains the 'new' command, which Jesus gave—the writer wishes to appeal directly to the expression in GJ, for that too is part of the heritage. And certainly, for him, it retained its novelty and freshness when he compared the life of the community with that of the surrounding world. Still, there has been a change from Gospel to Epistle: the 'new' of GJ xiii. 34 signified the newness of the dispensation brought by Christ—the coming of the End into the midst. That sense is no longer so prominent. Rather, the word is retained largely out of tradition. The perspective is now temporal rather than qualitative. So the 'old' also comes into view, as antiquity—the link with origins—now means authority. This factor carries more weight than the sheer conviction that God acts.

But the presence and vitality (the newness) of the command to love is the evidence that **the darkness is passing away** (ii. 8), and it links God (or Jesus) with his followers, who are the objects of his love (*v.* 5). Despite his temporal perspective, he knows that **the genuine light is already shining**, that is in the coming of Christ or perhaps, rather, the message which he brought: for **God is light**, and Jesus carried the message which **we heard** (i. 5). In that sense, the End, God's decisive act of salvation, is already present and accessible.

Momentarily, indeed, in ii. 6 (**as he walked**), there is a reference, unique in 1J, apart from v. 6, to Jesus' lifetime (though cf. the historical-cum-doctrinal reference ·to his sinlessness in ii. 1 and iii. 6). The reference of 'he' slides from God to Jesus (it is *ekeinos*, which often designates Jesus in 1J, cf. p. 117), and we are reminded of statements such as GJ xiii. 15; xv. 9: the love demanded of the disciple is that which marked Jesus' own conduct, and he is its pattern.

A few points of detail remain. 'To perfect' (ii. 5) or bring to a consummation (*teleioō*) is a favourite Johannine word (cf. especially GJ xix. 28, 30), as is the general theme of the utter completeness of the action of God in Jesus, cf. GJ i. 17; iii. 34. The word is closely related to 'fulfil', *plēroō* (i. 4). Both belong to the vocabulary of eschatological hope. The Christian community is conscious that God's time of fulfilment has dawned, and this means the attainment of all aspects of his purpose: so his love finds full expression in those who keep his commands. **The love of God** must mean here God's love for man, not man's for God. The relationship between divine and human love remains to be explored (cf. iv. 16 ff.), here the moral life is seen straightforwardly as the evidence that a man is perfectly endowed with God's love.

It is clear how integral the moral teaching is to the Gospel message in this writer's eyes. The term **word** (*logos*), which in i. 1 he used to mean the whole Christian teaching, appears in ii. 5 as synonymous with God's commands, and the identification is confirmed in ii. 7. The régime of love is hardly distinguishable for this writer from the faith that God is light and wholly free from darkness; for that too is **the message** (*angelia*).

The only textual uncertainty of any importance in this passage is in i. 7, where some quotations of the verse by Church fathers, one Old Latin manuscript and one important Greek codex (A) replace **each other** by 'him' (i.e. God). Either accords with the general thought of the writer; 'him' is the word more naturally expected in the context (cf. *v.* 6), while **each other** introduces a fresh idea. While the symmetry of the passage makes 'him' the more likely original (cf. O'Neill, op. cit., p. 10), scribes may well have abandoned **each other** in the interests of simplification or out of careless imitation of *v.* 6.

### 3. THE CHRISTIAN CAUSE
### ii. 12-17

**(12) I write to you, children, because your sins are removed on account of his name. (13) I write to you, fathers, because you have known him who is from the beginning. I write to you, young men, because you have overcome the Evil One. (14) I have written to you, little ones, because you know the Father. I have written to you, fathers, because you know him who is from the beginning. I have written to you, young men, because you are strong and the word of God dwells in you and you have overcome the Evil One. (15) Do not love the world or that which is in it. If a man loves the world, the love of the Father is not in him; (16) for everything that is in the world, the desire of the flesh and the desire of the eyes, and pride about possessions—all this is not from the Father but from the world. (17) And both the world and its desires are transient. But he who does God's will abides for ever.**

We isolate this short section because it forms a solemn, direct and, to all appearances, self-contained address by our writer to his readers. Here perhaps, more than elsewhere in the Epistle, he speaks to them in the words demanded by the time of writing, without relying on existing material; and here more than elsewhere the readers are marshalled before us in their several categories—even if it is not wholly clear what the categories signify. The section also contains a strong statement of the writer's outlook on the universe. In *vv.* 15–16 it is revealed at its most pessimistic. Moreover, this passage, when viewed in terms of its place in the work as a whole, forms a bridge between i. 5–ii. 11, where the writer lays out many of his leading ideas, and ii. 18 ff., where he enters the lists much more explicitly against the deviants.

He is very close to his readers and writes to them in the warm terms of the pastor confident of the love and respect of at least the greater part of his flock. This is not his first direct address to them: he calls them his **children** (*teknia*) in ii. 1 and his **dear ones** (*agapētoi*) in ii. 7. Both terms are used repeatedly—the former seven times (cf. GJ xiii. 33), the latter six. They are our writer's favourites.

Now, however, we have a succession of other terms of address in brief space: **fathers, young men, little ones**. The sentences fall into two sets of three—the structure is deliberate and formal.[1] Each trio has the same order, though the word used for the first group differs in the two cases—*teknia*, **children** (*v.* 12) is exchanged, for no very clear reason, for **little ones**, *paidia* (*v.* 14; cf. also ii. 18), whose meaning is not significantly different. It is not easy to decide who are designated by the three titles. Are they three sections of the congregation? In view of the frequent use of **children** elsewhere in the Epistle as a general address, it is more likely that **fathers** and **young men** are the leading groups within the community, while **children** (and **little ones**) signifies the congregation as a whole. Unlike the Pauline congregations, where women played an important part, this Johannine church accords them no prominence. It is another sign of its Jewish quality; as is the use, with its rabbinic parallels, of 'children' and the like for the ordinary members of the group, cf. the use of *mikroi* ('little ones'), probably with this meaning, in the Gospel of Matthew (x. 42; xviii. 6, 10, 14).

How formal are these titles? Are **fathers** and **young men** equivalents of the terms 'elders' (or, to give its more formal English equivalent, 'presbyters', Acts xx. 17; Titus i. 5) and 'servants' (or 'deacons', Phil. i. 1; 1 Tim. iii. 8 ff.), which were coming to be used elsewhere as customary titles for the presiding group and the servants or assistants of the community and its leaders (cf. also the letters of Ignatius of Antioch, *ECW*, pp. 73 ff.)? Or are they less formal and official than that? In view of the signs of concern with the discipline and organization of the community

[1] For this triple form, cf. Jewish parallels, e.g. Pirke Aboth i. 1, 2, 6, 7; Charles, II, pp. 691 f.

shown in the Johannine Epistles, it is likely that the terms possess some degree of formality. We need not be surprised if the Johannine church used titles other than those used elsewhere, though it is not without interest that these were not the titles which eventually won general currency. It is perhaps a measure of the 'off-centre' quality of Johannine Christianity at this time that others soon came to prevail in the Church at large.

If we are right in taking these words as the designations of church officials, then at least on one aspect of the matter a plausible suggestion can be made. The title 'elder' does not appear for officers of the congregation because, as 2J 1 and 3J 1 indicate, in Johannine nomenclature it signifies a figure whose supervisory role extends, from outside, over, probably, a number of dependent congregations (cf. pp. 4 f.).

As the alteration from *teknia* to *paidia* (*v.* 12 and *v.* 14) is no more than stylistic, so probably is the change from **I write** to **I wrote** in the second triplet (*v.* 14). It is certainly hard to believe that the second set is taken from an earlier writing; and if the past tense does have force it is odd to put the statements in that tense after those in the present. It is much more likely that this is a case of the epistolary aorist, a common Greek (and Latin) convention, in which the writer puts himself into the position of the reader, for whom, when he comes to read the letter, the writing is a past event. Its use alongside the present remains strange. In the absence of any clear evidence that the transmission or composition of this passage has been mishandled in some way (on the contrary, in general it hangs together particularly well), it is best to conclude that this idiom has been employed, simply for the sake of diversifying the style, but used inexpertly.[1]

All six statements are best read as encapsulations, suitable for the time, of the writer's essential and no doubt well-known convictions. Unlike most of 1J's direct assertions, they contain neither repetition by parallel statement nor antithesis. They stand out by reason of their solemnity and their form. Nevertheless, they are not in the least an interruption of the argument: they look back particularly to *v.* 8. As always, while using, we believe, distinct items of material, our writer is careful to make connections. Here he presents the assured signs in the Christian brothers that the

[1] Cf. C. F. D. Moule, *An Idiom-book of New Testament Greek*, Cambridge, 1963, p. 12.

era of darkness is being superseded, now that the true light shines.

No ingenuity has been spared by scholars in trying to find how each of the benefits of life in the dispensation brought by Christ is appropriate to the category of persons with which it is linked. If, as we suppose, **children** (v. 12) represents the community as a whole, then forgiveness of sins fits admirably (cf. i. 7; ii. 2), for it is both general and fundamental. Similarly, the ideas of victory in fight and strength (cf. v. 4 f.) are suitably associated with the young members of the church (v. 13 and v. 14). And it is not inappropriate that the senior members, concerning whom the same statement is made twice, should be particularly conscious of the origins and heritage of the Christian movement. The Christ they have come to know is **from the beginning**; and here, perhaps, the sense of that word in twofold—it refers to the beginning of the preaching of the Gospel and (more clearly) to the beginning of all things (cf. GJ i. 1; see also pp. 48 f.). It is not clear why knowing the Father should have been selected for the second address to the community as a whole. We do best to take it as evidence for the great importance given by this writer to 'knowing' (cf. p. 65), and are reminded of the key statement using this word in GJ xvii. 3. Nevertheless, it is noteworthy that forgiveness of sins takes precedence (cf. i. 7 ff.). Once more, our writer's interest is both theological and ethical, both speculative and practical. But the ethical has the edge. He gives no hint of approval to enlightenment which might leave man's moral state untreated.

The conquest of the Evil One (*ponēros*) was, in the eyes of the first Christians, one of the chief results of Christ's work. The way in which his death, regarded as the occasion of the conflict, brought about that defeat is nowhere stated clearly in the literature included in the New Testament, though myths about it were soon to develop; but the belief itself is amply attested (1 Cor. ii. 8; Col. ii. 15; Rom. viii. 31-9). **The Evil One** is a Johannine term for the devil, cf. iii. 12; v. 18; GJ xvii. 15; see also 2 Thess. iii. 3; Eph. vi. 16. We may compare with the Johannine confidence that the Evil One has been vanquished (cf. v. 18), the sense of continuing battle among the men of Qumran (and in the New Testament, cf. Eph. vi. 10 ff.): even though 'the children of righteousness are ruled by the Prince of Light', yet 'the Angel of Darkness leads (them) astray, and until his end, all their sin, iniquities, wickedness, and

all their unlawful deeds are caused by his dominion' (1QS iii,
Vermes, pp. 75 f.). They live still in the thick of the conflict,
whereas for the Johannine Christians, Christ has conquered, GJ
xvi. 33; 1J iii. 8.

In *vv.* 15–17, we have a wide general statement of the writer's
'philosophy'. The tenuous connection with what precedes and
follows has led some scholars (e.g. Bultmann) to the view that
these verses come from the last stage in the composition of the
work. Read in isolation, they witness to a more extreme dualist
position than the Epistle as a whole. The heretics would have
found them wholly congenial (see also p. 15). Only v. 19 expresses
such a deep pessimism about the world and its affairs. Moreover,
some of the words do not appear elsewhere. Even so, it is loving
the world, not living in it, which is condemned—the accent,
typically, is ethical (cf. James iv. 4). However, these verses are not
wholly uncharacteristic of the Epistle's attitude to the world; cf.
iii. 1, 13, 17; iv. 4 f.; v. 4 f.; it is only a question of accent. And
they may be read alongside similar statements in the Gospel,
where however there are more 'positive' statements to balance
them, e.g. GJ xvii. 9, 16, as against iii. 17 (cf. p. 63 n.). As we
have already suggested, the specific aim of this passage is to state
fundamentals baldly and sharply.

In *v.* 15, there is a problem of interpretation. Is a contrast being
drawn between two loves, one of which a man must choose—love
for God or for the world? Or is the genitive (**of the Father**) sub-
jective, so that the sense is that if a man loves the world, it can be
taken as proof that God's love has not come to dwell within him?
There is no difficulty in taking the former view: that man can—
and should—love God is a familiar idea in this work, cf. iv. 20;
v. 2 f.; and it makes good sense of the imperative in *v.* 15, **Do not
love the world.** For on the second view, God's indwelling love
appears as a gift which may be bestowed or withheld, and there
seems little scope for responding to a command. The task is simply
to receive the gift if it appears, and there is little a man can do if
he is not brought within the circle of recipients. Nevertheless, the
use of the expression a few verses earlier, in ii. 5, was almost
certainly in this second sense, and the phrase **from the Father**
(*v.* 16) tallies with it. The thought is of God as a source—of love and
not of evil. Further support comes from the fact that in *v.* 17, the
writer avoids 'he who loves God', which we should expect, in

favour of **he who does God's will**.[1] And as for the imperative in *v.* 15, we are in the familiar area (not confined to Johannine thought, cf. Gal. v. 25), where Christian status, resulting from God's gift in and through Christ, is recognizable from and attested by moral behaviour for which a man must strive, cf. iv. 10.

The distinction between **desire of the flesh** and **desire of the eyes** is not immediately apparent. 'Flesh' is probably used in the wide, Jewish sense which it bears so commonly in the writings of Paul (e.g. Rom. viii. 3 ff.; Gal. v. 19): it signifies all the sinful tendencies of man. It is true that the two other uses of the word in the Johannine Epistles (1J iv. 2; 2J 7) have a simpler, non-ethical meaning—simply bodily life—but a sense closer to ours is in GJ viii. 15. **The desire of the eyes** probably stands more narrowly for greed and lust. The final expression in the triad, meaning literally 'pride of life', is best taken to refer to arrogance and rash confidence concerning worldly goods: it is a reasonably common sense of *bios* ('life'), occurring again in iii. 17 (cf. our use of 'livelihood'). So **the desire of the eyes** and **pride in possessions** are twin aspects of the general **desire of the flesh**. The attack on concern with property is a motif found in a wide range of New Testament writers, above all Luke (vi. 20; Acts iv. 32–v. 11; cf. James i. 9, 11; Mark x. 23 ff.). The triad finds an almost complete parallel in the roughly contemporary Jewish document, the Damascus Rule. In iv. 17 f. are listed 'the three nets of Satan with which Levi son of Jacob said that he catches Israel by setting them up as three kinds of righteousness. The first is riches, the second is fornication, and the third is profanation of the Temple' (Vermes, p. 101). It is not surprising that our writer, both Christian and in any case non-Palestinian, lacks the cultic interest; but for the rest the two works coincide.[2]

The verb translated **are transient** (*v.* 17) is the same as that rendered **is passing away** in *v.* 8. That may not be quite the sense here. Though the writer believes that the world is indeed passing away, his point in this verse is to draw a contrast between that

---

[1] J. Coppens, in *Ephemerides Theologicae Lovanienses*, 45, 1969, pp. 125–7, takes the opposite view. God's love for man is referred to only in iii. 16, 17 and iv. 2. It is a question of man's love for God, he holds, not only in the obvious passages, iv. 20 f., and v. 1–3, but also in ii. 5; ii. 17; and iv. 12—in addition to our present passage.

[2] On this verse, cf. N. Lazure, *Revue Biblique*, 76, 1969, pp. 161 ff.

which abides and that which does not. We note both the longing
for durable, eternal salvation, so characteristic of the religious
aspiration of the period, and the moral basis on which, in this
writer's belief, it can alone be grounded. The 'mystical', super-
natural gift of God's love had certainly to be received (*v.* 15)—but
the test of that was no mere spiritual 'feeling'; it was doing God's
will, the keeping of his commands, in particular the command to
love the brothers (v. 2 f.).

## 4. CHRIST OR ANTICHRIST
### ii. 18-27

(18) Little ones, it is the last hour. You have heard that Antichrist is coming: well, now many antichrists have appeared.
That is how we know that it is the last hour. (19) They went
out from our society—but they did not truly belong to us.
For if they had belonged to us, they would have stayed with
us. (Their going out was) to show that not all members of our
society are really part of us. (20) You too have an anointing
from the Holy One and you all have knowledge. (21) I have
not written to you as people who do not know the truth but
precisely because you do know it, and because no lie has any
part with the truth. (22) Who then is the liar? It is the man
who denies that Jesus is the Messiah. Is not this man the
Antichrist—he who denies the Father and the Son? (23) He
who denies the Son has no hold on the Father either. He who
acknowledges the Son possesses the Father too. (24) Make
sure that what you have heard from the beginning dwells in
you. If what you have heard from the beginning does indeed
dwell in you, then you yourselves dwell in the Son and in the
Father. (25) And this is what he himself promised to us—
eternal life. (26) I have written this to you about those who
are leading you astray. (27) And remember that the anointing
which you received from him dwells in you, and you have
no need for anyone to be your teacher. But his anointing
itself teaches you about everything, and is true and not false.
And as he has taught you, so dwell in him.

At this point, the opponents, those of whom the pastor's flock is to beware, begin to come more clearly into view. From now on we see something of their relationship to the rest of the Christian body and rather more of their beliefs and (in the writer's view) inadequacies and heresies.

Taking up, on this occasion alone, the word he used in *v.* 14, he addresses his **little ones** (*paidia*): he reverts to his usual **children** (*teknia*) in *v.* 28. He begins with what is in effect a syllogism, whose simple logic satisfies him. The coming of the Antichrist will be a sign that the last hour has arrived; Antichrist has come (in multiple form); therefore **it is the last hour**. He is so sure of his reasoning that he announces the conclusion first.

It goes without saying that the opening of this section confirms the Jewish orientation of this work. We have already noted (in relation to i. 7 and ii. 2) elements of a more commonplace Judaistic background to the Christianity expressed here than that found in the Gospel of John. Here is another sign of this lower level of sophistication. In GJ, the conventional Jewish pattern of eschatology occupies a relatively small place—just a few references to coming judgement and resurrection at the Last Day (v. 28 f.; vi. 39, 40, 44; xii. 48)—and the weight falls almost wholly on what God has already done in Christ; that has the significance of the expected decisive intervention of God at the End, and the ideas associated with the End in Judaism are linked with Jesus (e.g. iii. 17-19; v. 24; xi. 25). This crucial and creative theological development is not carried through into 1J with anything like the same thoroughness. It is true that **the light is already shining** (ii. 8), but it is not wholly clear that this does not refer to the Gospel message rather than to Jesus himself as the decisive agent of God. And we have already noted both the attention to the message in preference to the messenger in 1J i. 1-4 (by contrast with the prologue of the Gospel) and the relative lack of advanced ideas about the person of Jesus. It is not unfair to say that for this writer, Jesus had appeared as the messianic messenger and the remover of sins whose coming both assured and foreshadowed the End. So it is true that he conquered the Evil One and enabled his followers to share in that victory (ii. 13), just as he brought a word that confers eternal life (i. 1 f.). But for our writer, these things seem not to represent the End in its fullness, but rather the beginning of the End. The coming of Christ set in train the events that would lead inevitably to that conclusion, and now **the last hour** has arrived. In line with this, Jesus' own return is expected (ii. 28). The indication that the eschatology has returned to a more conventional pattern is that the sign of the End is not some aspect of the state of life which Christ inaugurated, but the external fact that opposition to the (orthodox) message has reached a climax. Eschatology is determined not, as in GJ, by a wide-ranging sense of God's saving gift of eternal life having been planted within the world, but by the outward circumstances of the Church. From Daniel onwards, in both Jewish and then Christian apocalypses, the trials and persecutions of the elect had been an essential pointer to the nearness of the final crisis; as had the clear emergence of sides and issues—exactly the situation in the Johannine church (cf. Col. i. 24; Mark xiii; Matt. xiii. 30).

This remained a stock feature of Jewish expectation. In successive revolts against Roman power, culminating in the Bar Cochba rebellion of A.D. 135, the ferocity of the enemy's attack was always seen as the signal for hope that God would bare his arm and reveal his power. The crisis which has now arisen for this Christian group is, to the outward eye, of small dimensions; it is the emergence within the community itself of men who oppose what the writer sees as the fundamental articles of the Gospel—chiefly, that Jesus is the Messiah (see also iv. 2; 2J 7). But so firm is his conviction that Jesus is God's chosen agent for carrying out his purposes in the world that this development, affecting, as far as we can see, only his own immediate Christian group, is seen as sufficient evidence that the cosmic catastrophe is about to take place. No wonder the range of ideas in the Epistle is narrow and no wonder we have just had such a succinct statement of fundamental matters. It is a time for slogans rather than diffuse or leisured argument.

Antichrist has come—in the shape of the heretics: **many antichrists.** The word may well be of the writer's own coinage; there is no earlier occurrence. Jesus is Messiah (*v.* 22)—the heretics are 'anti-messiahs'. Usage in the case of comparable words (*antitheos*, 'anti-god'; *anti-stratēgos*, 'anti-general') suggests that they are seen less as opponents than as usurpers and deceivers (cf. *v.* 26). The underlying idea of the devil or his champion ranging himself against God and his chosen agents is of course a commonplace: in the New Testament, cf. Rev. xii. 10; Mark iii. 22 ff.; 2 Thess.

ii. 3 f. We cannot be sure, but this expectation of an imminent End may well have been a crucial factor dividing the writer's friends from his opponents. For the latter, perhaps, the old Johannine teaching remained and had been carried further—the End, with its attendant enjoyment of sinlessness and eternal life (p. 16), had fully come. The fevered speculation of 'the orthodox' may well have seemed a lamentably retrograde development into simple religion.

The heretics have gone into schism. It is worth noting that as far as our documents go, this is a new development. There is ample evidence of doctrinal disagreement already in the Pauline congregations, sometimes on crucial matters (e.g. 1 Cor. xv, concerning resurrection; Galatians, concerning the law), but nowhere do we find any hint (except in the case of an individual, and the issue is moral not doctrinal, 1 Cor. v. 1 ff.) of expulsion or separation from the fellowship. But now—and it is the shape of things to come—in this Johannine church at least, the lines of orthodoxy have become too rigid to tolerate divergent views, though it seems that it was the heretics who could no longer tolerate the rest rather than the other way round (**they went out**, *v.* 19). This development is all the more striking in that on many matters (such as their negative attitude to the world) no more than a hair's breadth can have divided the parties and it is never made clear why, in the writer's doctrinal scheme, the question of Jesus' full human life is of such moment (cf. pp. 35 f.). There is a hint of some embarrassment on this matter in *v.* 19: what clinches the judgement that the opponents do not belong in one community with the orthodox is that **they have gone out**—not, in the last resort, erroneous belief.[1] (Is Judas their prototype, cf. GJ xiii.30?)

The situation is accepted as foreordained; it had to happen. **They did not truly belong to us. For if they had belonged to us, they would have stayed with us.** Their very departure is proof that they belong in the other camp. The determinism is simple, and again it is part of the perspective of conventional eschatology. As the End draws near, wheat and tares will be sifted, God will winnow the corn (cf. Mark iv. 11 f.; Matt. xiii. 30, 49 f.). It applies also to the writer's friends. Their position is equally

[1] In *v.* 19, the writer plays nicely on the dual sense of the preposition *ex*: 'of' meaning both 'out of' and 'part of'. So, literally, 'They went out of us, but they were not (part) of us.'

objective. They have received an anointing from God and attained thereby knowledge of the truth (cf. iii. 9).[1]

Ethical considerations are usually prominent in this work, but here (as indeed in other passages) membership of the 'sphere' of God seems to be simply a matter of God's arbitrary choice and the question of moral record is not raised, though no doubt that is meant to conform.

**The Holy One** (*v.* 20) usually signifies God in Jewish usage, and that is the reference here; but cf. GJ vi. 65, where Jesus is described as the Holy One of God.

'Anointing' might almost be seen as the *leitmotiv* of the first part of this passage. The crucial point of faith is to hold that Jesus is the anointed one ( = Messiah = *Christos*); the opponents are in effect opponents of Jesus, and so *antichristoi*; the faithful supporters of Jesus have (like him—in his baptism?) received an anointing (*chrisma*) from God, *vv.* 20 and 27. The idea occurs in a comparable way in 2 Cor. i. 22, and in both passages it is likely that baptism is in mind as the occasion when the anointing is conferred. In later times, literal anointing came to be a ceremony linked with baptism, and it gained particular currency in Gnostic sects. But there is no evidence that this was the case at this early stage, and the parallel use of the image of divine seed in iii. 9 indicates that we have here not a reference to a rite but a verbal scheme which arose in the manner we have indicated—from the conviction that Jesus was the Messiah. From *v.* 27 it appears that the idea of anointing is to be 'cashed' chiefly in terms of teaching: to be anointed is to have received a doctrine. There is a similar use of the idea in Ignatius' Letter to the Ephesians xvii (*ECW*, p. 80): 'You must never let yourselves be anointed with the malodorous chrism of the prince of this world's doctrines.'[2]

In *v.* 21, the expression of the contrast between the two groups shifts from membership of or separation from the fellowship to truth versus falsehood. Already in ii. 4, the description 'liar' has been given to those who claim knowledge of God and fail to

---

[1] Some manuscripts and ancient versions go further in a 'Gnostic' direction and alter *pantes* to *panta* (*v.* 20)—**you all have knowledge** to 'you know all things'; cf. ii. 27. The variant may be an assimilation to the later verse, or genuine, the two statements being parallel.

[2] For an examination of unction in initiation, which the writer thinks may have been already current in the practice of the Johannine church, see W. Nauck, *Die Tradition und der Charakter des ersten Johannesbriefes*, pp. 147 ff.

observe his (or Christ's) commands. Now two developments take place. The 'liars' are in schism; and their fault is one not only of morals but also of faith (cf. iii. 23). They do not accept Jesus as Messiah. The two are linked in that it is because Jesus is Messiah that his commands have authority. It is now clearer than in ii. 4 that to lie is not to say what one knows to be untrue, but to fail to hold what the writer believes to be the truth.

The false belief goes a stage further. To deny the Son is to deny the Father. The reasoning which warrants this statement is not laid out. Perhaps (like the play with *christos*) it has a verbal basis: Jesus is not only Messiah, he can also be called God's Son (cf. v. 5) —that is by this time a datum of Christian terminology, and indeed the title belongs to the story which was perhaps seen as his anointing (Mark i. 11). Maybe there was enough in the Jewish background to make the two titles synonymous. Certainly they were so in Johannine usage, cf. GJ i. 41, 49; xi. 27; xx. 31. 'Son' implies 'father'—the one carries the other with it. Hence to deny the one is necessarily to deny the other—and so to be deprived of him (*v.* 23). At a deeper level—which the words bring along with them—to have a false belief in God's agent is to have a false belief in God himself. And if you do not 'possess' the Son you cannot 'possess' the Father who mediates himself uniquely through the Son. To refuse the Son is to refuse the Father whose accredited agent he is.

'Denial' takes two forms. There is denial of the fact that Jesus is the Messiah. There is also denial of the Son. The first is a failure in accepting knowledge, of hold upon the truth. The second is a failure of allegiance. The first failure labels one a liar; and its antithesis is, presumably, to tell the truth. The opposite of the second kind of denial is to confess or acknowledge (*v.* 23), that is to affirm belief or attachment. But the two forms of denial run into each other, because belief that Jesus is the Messiah carries with it, as far as this writer is concerned, attachment to him and his cause. It is not simply an acceptance of the factual correctness of the assertion.

The statements in *v.* 23 do not run as we should expect on the basis of comparable Johannine passages such as GJ v. 23; xv. 23; the parallelism is imperfect. Instead of 'he who denies (or confesses) the Son denies (or confesses) the Father too', we have the introduction of the verb *to have*. Denial (or affirmation) of the Son determines one's possession of or hold upon the Father. In the

Gospel (apart from i. 20), the idea of denial of Christ occurs only in the case of Peter in the Passion of Jesus (xiii. 38; xviii. 25, 27). How prominent this terrible incident was in Christians' minds, including that of the writer of this Epistle, so that it is in mind here, we cannot know. The story of Peter's self-exclusion from fellowship with Christ, albeit temporarily, may well have been the stock instance of apostasy under the pressure of opposition.

However, there is no hint that the circumstances in which denial or confession of Christ are creating division among the members of the Johannine church involve persecution from outside. The situation is one of controversy among Christians not of witness in the presence of outsiders. (Contrast the use of the same words in the setting of persecution in Matt. x. 32 f.; Luke xii. 8 f.) It is perhaps another mark of that self-preoccupation of the Johannine community, of which we have other signs (e.g. the ethic of love of the Christian brothers, cf. p. 63).

The idea of possessing God has no parallel in GJ, but occurs again in 2J 9 (cf. 1J v. 12). It came to have currency in Gnostic circles. Certainly it has in it all the possibilities of man's manipulation of the divine which was a strong tendency of the Gnostic mentality; and it easily eliminates that firm sense of the saving initiative and freedom of God which may be thought essential to an authentic Jewish or Christian perspective. There is certainly no lack of emphasis in 1J on that divine initiative (e.g. ii. 25, 27; iv. 9, 19); but the use of this expression, absent from GJ, is, like the strong 'anti-world' statements (p. 15), one of those puzzling signs that our writer was very close to the thought of his opponents in some of his basic assumptions and that his case against them was far from being worked out with complete consistency.

In v. 24, the writer returns implicitly to the idea of the truth (cf. v. 21), this time linking it clearly to the content of his message— **what you have heard from the beginning**. As in ii. 7, 13, 14 and iii. 11, he appeals to the continuous identity of the Christian tradition: one of the most powerful arguments in favour of its authenticity, an argument which was to be appealed to more and more, by heretics as well as by the orthodox (for the former, cf. Ptolomaeus, 'Letter to Flora', in R. M. Grant, *Gnosticism*, London, 1961, p. 190), as doctrinal disagreement became sharper and the search for authorities more urgent.

As in GJ (e.g. xv. 4-10) **dwell** (*menō, vv.* 24, 27) is a word of great power. Though the traditional translation, 'abide', is largely archaic, it catches the sense of utter and dependable permanence which the writer wishes to give. In 1J it carries this strong sense in every case (it occurs twenty-three times) except ii. 19. It is one of the chief ways in which the ultimate quality inherent in membership of the domain of God or of 'the world' is conveyed (cf. iii. 9, 14).

In *v.* 25, **he** represents one of a number of emphatic uses of the pronoun *autos* (the subject of the verb, if pronominal, is usually left unexpressed in Greek). Other examples are in i. 7; ii. 2; iv. 10, 19. It always refers either to God or Christ; here it is unclear which is intended, and perhaps no distinction is drawn—both are mentioned in the preceding sentence. In Johannine thought, the one mediates the other, and the two are in unity (GJ x. 30). So the promise of eternal life (cf. i. 2) originates from the Father but has been communicated by the Son (cf. GJ x. 10; xvii. 2; xx. 31).

How far is the promise already fulfilled for the believers? Is **eternal life** already theirs—the life of the coming age present since Christ's coming—or is it life in the future? Our writer never decides, or rather he knows that it is both—and thereby probably distinguishes himself from the heretics who see themselves already in a perfected, sinless state (i. 8): see iii. 2 for both sides, and iii. 14 and v. 12 for statements implying that all has already been done. The inconsistency, as it appears, is much reduced by ii. 18: Christians are indeed *in via*, but the End is in sight.

There is little new in *vv.* 26 f. In the description of the heretics as **those who are leading you astray**, we have a sign of the effectiveness of their teaching and so of the seriousness of the threat which they pose. This Epistle is written to meet an emergency: it is by no means a gentle contribution to discussion. There may well be an element of hoping against hope in the confidence of the tone with which the pastor addresses his audience. So this reference to the opponents leads him to yet another assurance of the status of his friends: they are anointed by God and so have only to remain steady, in the enjoyment of the endowment which they have received. They have no need of any further teaching— they have all the truth they could possibly want. Let them remain safely inside their charmed circle and resist those who wish to teach them more. The anointing itself has conveyed truth to them —truth about everything (cf. the variant reading in ii. 20, p. 79 n.). This is the authentic Gnostic tone. The rivalry between the two groups concerns this knowledge of **everything** (cf. the claim of the Corinthian Christians in 1 Cor. viii. 1, accepted by Paul—with irony). What it covered, we cannot be sure; though we may suppose that for our writer it means those truths which his work expounds. Nothing else really mattered.

It is not without significance that 'the truth' can be described as something taught, and that the anointing is seen in these terms. We are in the presence of a doctrine transmitted in the Church and this emphasis is characteristic of the work; but the idea of care about the genuineness of teaching is found already in GJ vii. 17.

Can we tell from this passage what was the nature of the heretics' teaching? Is our writer stating their position fairly? From iv. 2, we know that they denied Christ's 'fleshness': they saw him, we may suppose, as a purely spiritual emissary from God (cf. pp. 34 f.). Here, however, we read that they denied his Messiahship. Was their fault that they would not accept this purely Jewish title and concept as suitable for Jesus their saviour? Did they prefer other, non-Jewish categories in which to conceive of him? Perhaps the division is between members of the congregation whose background lay in Judaism and those whose antecedents were pagan. If so, we should expect the second group to prefer titles like 'saviour' or 'lord', both of which in fact spanned the two cultures; the former at least was acceptable to our writer, iv. 14; cf. GJ iv. 42; and the latter never appears.

Much more likely, they can accept the title Messiah for their redeemer but will not identify him wholly with the fleshly, human Jesus: cf. iv. 2; v. 6; 2J 7. They believe in the Christ, but Jesus is not he. This for them is the stone of stumbling, and for our writer their belief is damnable heresy.

We may be sure that the other charge levelled against them, that they deny the Father and the Son (*v.* 22), would not be acceptable to them as a statement of their belief. This was how the matter seemed to the writer, but it was inference not exact reporting. What is clear is that the opponents still regard themselves as belonging to the Christian camp—enough to be attempting to convert the rest to their views (*v.* 26). They had indeed, in the writer's view, it appears, masqueraded as members of the 'true Church' for some time (*v.* 19)—until the true state of things had been revealed by their defection.

# 5. THE TWO FAMILIES
## ii. 28–iii. 24

(28) And now, children, dwell in him, so that when he is revealed we may have confidence and not be ashamed before him at his appearing. (29) If you know that he is righteous, then you know that everyone who does what is right is born of him. (iii. 1) See how great is the love which the Father has given to us so that we might be called God's offspring—and that is what we are. The reason the world does not recognize us is that it did not recognize him. (2) Loved ones, we are now God's offspring, and what we shall be has not yet been revealed. We know that when he is revealed we shall be like him, because we shall see him as he is. (3) Everyone who has this hope in him purifies himself as he is pure. (4) Everyone who commits sin also breaks the law—because sin is lawlessness. (5) And you are aware that he was revealed in order to remove sins, and there is no sin in him. (6) The man who dwells in him does not sin; the man who sins has neither seen nor known him. (7) Children, let no one lead you astray. The man who does the right is righteous, as he is righteous. (8) The man who commits sin springs from the devil, for the devil sins from the beginning. This is why the Son of God was revealed—to abolish the devil's works. (9) No one born of God commits sin, because his seed dwells in him; and he cannot sin because he is born of God. (10) In this way it is clear who are God's offspring and who are the devil's. Everyone who fails to do the right is no child of God—and the same goes for him who does not love his brother. (11) For this is the message which you heard from the beginning— that we should love one another. (12) Not like Cain who was born of the Evil One and murdered his brother. And why did he do that? Because his deeds were evil whereas his brother's were righteous. (13) Do not be surprised, brothers, if the world hates you. (14) We know that we have passed out of death into life, because we love the brothers. The man who does not love dwells in death. (15) Everyone who hates

his brother is a murderer, and you know that no murderer
has eternal life dwelling in him. (16) This is how we know
what love is—that he gave his life for us. And we for our part
ought to give our lives for the brothers. (17) How can the
love of God be present in a man who is wealthy, sees his
brother is in need and yet withholds his kindness from him?
(18) Children, let us not love simply in words or talk, but in
action and genuinely. (19) This is how we shall know that we
belong to the truth, and assure ourselves in his sight (20) that
even if our conscience condemns us, God is greater than our
conscience and knows everything. (21) My dear ones, if our
conscience does not condemn us, we can approach God
confidently, (22) and we receive from him whatever we ask
for because we keep his commands and do what he approves.
(23) This is his command: we are to believe in the name of
his Son, Jesus Christ, and we are to love each other just as he
commanded us. (24) The man who keeps his commands
dwells in God and God dwells in him. And we can tell that
he dwells in us from the Spirit which he has given to us.

The writer of 1J oscillates between two kinds of awareness of
the Christians' position in the world. On the one hand, there is the
virtually timeless state of affairs introduced by Christ characterized by such expressions as 'dwelling in the light' (ii. 10), or
'knowing the truth' (ii. 21). This is the dominant tone of GJ.
On the other hand, there is the sense that the End is near, and in
1J this is no less strong than the first kind of awareness. Yet his
theological vocabulary and stock of ideas belong chiefly to that
first category, and as he writes this standpoint continually comes
to the fore and takes charge. So from time to time he has to stop,
somewhat abruptly, to direct attention once more to the impending
crisis. This is what happened in ii. 18 (with *v.* 17 to a degree
preparing the way, with its reference to the transience of the
world's desires). It happens again in ii. 28, after the 'timeless'
pronouncements of ii. 23 ff. The **now** is probably deliberate:
'at this crucial time.' The same goes for the other uses of *nun*
in 1J (ii. 18; iii. 2; iv. 3).[1]

The general injunction of *v.* 27, to **dwell in him**, is now

[1] Bultmann, Commentary, p. 48, n. 3, takes the view that the word has no
temporal significance in these passages.

repeated with special force. There is a particular reason for sticking to Christ: that one may stand firm on the great day of his return. It was a common belief that this event would make the most stringent demands on his followers. It would be preceded and accompanied by unprecedented persecution and natural catastrophes. They would need every resource if they were to remain firm and loyal. Only after great tribulation would God's final victory be won. At least from the time of the Maccabean revolt this had been the pattern of Jewish expectation (cf. the Book of Daniel), and the Church, with the martyr-like death of Jesus at the heart of its message, had taken it over into its own belief about the future of the world (cf. Mark xiii, Luke xxi). So their constant fear was that they might fall into apostasy in the hour of crisis: they might **be ashamed**. And their prayer was for **confidence** (*v.* 28). Both terms are common in early Christian writing.

*Parrēsia*, **confidence**, appears four times in 1J, and the other occurrences illuminate the sense here. In iii. 21 and v. 14 it is a matter of boldness or confidence before God, and in iv. 17, as in our present passage, the occasion for its exercise is the day of Judgement. It is then a question of confidence in relation to God, not to men; but it was only possible to have that confidence if one maintained one's allegiance to God in the face of temptation to apostatize. (The word is used in GJ nine times, but not in this kind of context; for use comparable to that in our passage, see Eph. iii. 12; Heb. iv. 16; x. 19.)

'Having confidence' is virtually the same as 'not being ashamed before him'.[1] Again, God is the point of reference. It is in his presence that one wishes to be allowed to stand on the day of crisis and from whom one seeks a favourable verdict.

The same idea occurs in Phil. i. 20; and in the Gospels there is a related use of the word (or rather its compound, *epaischunō*)— only now the point of reference is not God but man. Christians may be ashamed, not now of themselves before God but of their faith in the presence of their persecutors: Mark viii. 38; Luke ix. 26. But the two uses of the word are linked, in that in these sayings we find that Jesus, seen as his followers' spokesman or advocate (cf. 1J ii. 1), will be ashamed, presumably before God, of those who were ashamed of him when subjected to attack. He will have

[1] The Greek means literally 'be ashamed from him', i.e. turn away in shame, cf. LXX Ecclus. xli. 17.

no ground on which to defend them and will be compelled to abandon them. In the language of 1J, they have 'denied'. (It is worth noting that as Peter, by his conduct during the Passion of Jesus, may be seen as the paradigm of denial, so he was, in Luke's telling of the story (though not in GJ), in the sequel ashamed before Christ, Luke xxii. 61 f.)

The way to ensure safety and acceptance on the great Day is to **dwell in him**. The word takes on an ethical flavour. In its characteristic Johannine use (see above, pp. 81 f.), it is full of theological profundity: it signifies that stable and assured relationship with God which the Christian has received, and it echoes with the permanence of eternity. 'To abide' is 'to be in Christ'. It is therefore hardly able to be used in the imperative mood. But here (as in the last clause of *v.* 27), it is so used, and while it appears to retain its full doctrinal meaning (as in ii. 10, 14, 24, 27), it has almost imperceptibly acquired a sense much more like 'persevere' (cf. the use of the related word, *hupomonē*, in Luke viii. 15; xxi. 19).

*Parousia* (**appearing**) is the usual word for the return of Christ (though it also means 'presence', e.g. Phil. ii. 12). This is its only Johannine occurrence, but cf. Matt. xxiv. 3; 1 Cor. xv. 23; 1 Thess. ii. 19 (see E. Best, *The First and Second Epistles to the Thessalonians*, London, 1972, pp. 349 ff.).

**When he is revealed**: the conjunction is *ean*, literally 'if'; but this suggests a doubt which is quite false to the intention. The use of the word in this sense is not uncommon, cf. iii. 21; GJ xii. 32; xiv. 3.

We now come to another of the frequent Johannine verbal chains (*v.* 29). What is true of the Father is true also of the Son, and becomes true of the believer. Here it is in terms of justice or righteousness (*dikaiosunē*). (As with the case of 'dwell' and 'abide' as renderings of *menō*, the archaic term, 'righteousness', is in some ways more successful in conveying the right sense, and because of the over-forensic flavour of 'justice' we have in our translation used this family of words.) We learnt in i. 9 that God is righteous and in ii. 1 that Jesus is righteous. Now, that being taken as accepted ground, there is the further step: **everyone who does what is right** (lit. 'does righteousness', cf. OT parallels, e.g. Ps. lxiii. 2, LXX, and Acts x. 35) **is born of him.** Born of whom? In the light of **his appearing**, we should expect it to be

87

Jesus; but, elsewhere (iii. 9; iv. 7; v. 1, 4), it must refer to God. Our writer slides easily from the one to the other, and it is impossible to be certain who is the subject of the verb **is** in the first part of the verse.

The link of thought with *v.* 28 is not brought to the surface. It is probably one more example of the moral reflex of this writer at work. If Christians are to have any ground for confidence at the coming of Christ, they must be God's true offspring, and that is made clear by (and in that sense at least depends upon) their moral rectitude. Morals are the sign and test that status is validly claimed. In iii. 7, **righteous** itself becomes a 'status' word, in a formulation parallel to that in ii. 29: being righteous corresponds to being **born of him**. So, in the later verse, it is not, as we might expect, that 'the righteous one does the right' but rather a man is shown to belong to the sphere of the right, that is God's sphere, by his right conduct.

The idea that Christians are God's offspring makes here its first appearance. It occupies a prominent place in the rest of 1J, especially in ch. v. Among early Christian writings it is not confined to this work alone. In the Johannine Gospel it is the leading theme of the opening section of ch. iii and appears in i. 12 and xi. 52; and it is found in Rom. viii. 14 ff.; Gal. iv. 5 f.; Matt. v. 9, 45; and, explicitly in connection with the idea of new birth, in 1 Peter i. 3, 23 and Tit. iii. 5. The 'seed' language of iii. 9 is sufficient indication that for our writer this is no loosely employed metaphor but that it is meant vividly and concretely. The writer is concerned not only with expressing the Christians' status in terms of sonship, but with the new birth which establishes it. So much is this the case that many scholars see in the use of this language evidence that baptism is in mind in these passages. GJ iii. 3 ff. and 1J v. 6 ff. give support to this view.

Our writer prefers to speak of Christians as 'born from God' or as 'children of God' than to give them the title accorded in the Pauline and Matthean passages referred to above—'sons'. Paul, characteristically, chooses the more daring expression: the believers receive the title which chiefly belongs to Christ. Though GJ (in xv. 14 f.) can make a comparably striking point when Christians are described by Jesus as no longer servants but friends, the title 'son' is reserved exclusively for Christ himself. As in the Epistle to the Hebrews (ch. i), where it is used to distinguish Jesus from the angels, the title has become more of a technical term, to denote him alone.

The idea of God's people as his sons or children is of course no invention of the New Testament. Israel as a whole is spoken of as God's son in Hosea xi. 1, as is the king in particular in 2 Sam. vii. 14 and Psalm ii. 7. It is indeed a commonplace of religion. A Christian writer can quote a pagan poet's (Aratus) use of it in Acts xvii. 28. The extension of the concept to focus on the fact of rebirth is typical of the concern in our period with salvation: how vital it was by some means to bring about one's transference to the secure domain of the redeemed, and how important therefore the process or act by which that transfer could be achieved. It is a dominant theme in the later Gnostic writings and, to take a prominent example, in the third-century Corpus Hermeticum. The affinities of this side of Johannine religion and certainly its future development lay in this direction.[1]

That Christians enjoy this status is the result of God's love (cf. iv. 19). Salvation is wholly the result of his initiative: man is helpless to save himself. What is more, to be God's child is seen in quite definite and physical terms: God's seed is in Christians (iii. 9). It is as objective as the anointing of ii. 20.

It looks from this passage as if 'God's offspring' (*tekna theou*) may have been in Johannine circles a title which Christians were proud of and to which they had become accustomed: they are urged to be sure to take it literally (iii. 1). The concept carries with it a corollary: the objective division of mankind (not explicitly here all men, but at least those in the writer's purview) into two 'families'. This is by no means unparalleled. It was meat and drink to the Gnostic sects to be an élite among a doomed race, and we are very close to the division found in the Dead Sea Scrolls into the sons of light and the sons of darkness. There the thought is even more deterministic: men are in the power of either the angel of light or of the devil (cf. 1QS iii. 22, Vermes, p. 76).

So here once more, the dualism of 1J comes to the fore. It is

[1] See especially Corp. Herm. XIII, ed. Nock and Festugière, II, Paris, 1945, pp. 200 f. This extract shows the closeness of 1J to the thought of the later Hellenistic work: 'What manner of man is he that is brought into being by the Rebirth?—He that is born by that birth is another; he is a god and son of God. He is the All, and is in all; for he has no part in corporeal substance; he partakes of the substance of things intelligible, being wholly composed of powers of God.'

because they belong to God that the world does not know or **recognize** (lit. 'know') the Christians. It is unable to understand them because, by definition, it lacks the essential key—knowledge of the truth (ii. 21), or, in terms of iii. 1, knowledge of God. To know the father is to know the child—and the contrary is equally true (cf. Matt. xi. 27). So, conversely, the non-recognition by the world is the sign that the believers truly are God's children.

The second sentence in iii. 1 may be more closely connected with the first than the translation we have adopted suggests. It begins with the conjunction *dia touto*, literally 'because of this', or 'therefore'. This occurs not infrequently in sentences of this type, notably in GJ v. 16, 18; xii. 39. In these three examples, 'this' (*touto*) clearly looks ahead to the clause which gives the reason for the statement in the main clause. On grounds of Johannine style, then, we have taken the sense to be (literally): 'On account of *this* the world does not know us—that it did not know him.' But it may be that in this case, the conjunction looks to the preceding sentence, so that it runs: 'Therefore the world does not know us,[1] because it did not know him.' The force of 'therefore' is not, however, luminously clear.

The next verse (iii. 2) presents a problem of punctuation. It has usually been translated as in our version, but it is possible that it should be taken thus: 'Now we are offspring of God, and he has not yet been revealed. What we shall be we know, because if (*or* when) he is revealed we shall be like him....' It can be said in favour of this arrangement that there is no other use of the verb *phaneroō* ('reveal') in either 1J or GJ where the subject is the impersonal 'it'. Elsewhere it is God, Christ, life or love. Moreover, it eliminates the formal contradiction between not knowing **what we shall be** and knowing **that we shall be like him**. On the other hand, to take **what we shall be** as the object of the verb **we know**, and to take *hoti* after that verb as 'because' rather than **that**, are both pieces of syntactical gymnastics. (For this suggested rearrangement, see F. C. Synge, *JTS*, 3, 1952, p. 79.)

The point of the verse follows from ii. 28 and answers the question, What will happen to the believers on the day of Christ's return? (Given the context, it must refer to this and not to the

---

[1] For the sake of the sense, the variant 'you' is not to be preferred, even though it is well attested and is undoubtedly the harder text. For the reason for the large number of variants in pronouns, cf. p. 54.

death of individual Christians; cf. the quite different emphasis of GJ xiv. 1 ff.) Already they are God's offspring: what will this mean when the End comes? That secret has not yet been revealed. It is true that the sense may be as weak as 'it has not become clear' (cf. perhaps ii. 19), but more probably the writer sees it as a divine mystery which will be disclosed at the proper time. Paul spoke of this very matter in these terms (1 Cor. xv. 50 f.) and believed that he had been granted knowledge of it: there would be a sudden transformation of those Christians still alive at that Day, while the Christian dead would be raised. But for our writer it still lies hidden. Nevertheless, he is confident of one thing that bears on the matter: **we shall be like him**. 'Him' almost certainly refers to Christ, who is himself the Son of God—and so like God. Just as in ii. 29 the subject shifted from Christ (**at his appearing**, ii. 28) to God, so now, again without clear indication, it seems to shift back to Christ. This obscurity of reference has a backing in Johannine thought: 'He who has seen me has seen the Father' (GJ xiv. 9). In fact the idea of seeing God himself is not unparalleled in early Christian thought: cf. Matt. v. 8 and possibly Heb. xii. 14. Nevertheless, both the reference to the 'coming' in ii. 28 and the aspiration to be 'like him' are much more readily understandable of Christ than of God. (For the latter idea, see Rom. viii. 29.)

Both the contemporary mysticism, soon to come to such rich expression in the Gnostic sects, and the deeper Jewish background by no means rule out the idea of becoming like God. In Gen. i. 26, Adam is made in God's image, and Paul had seen Christ as the one in whom this was fully realized. Similarly, with a logic like that of our present passage, Paul had expressed the believers' relationship with Christ in terms of exposure to his glory leading to transformation into his likeness. Only for Paul, as distinct from this writer as he uses this idea, the exposure and the change are already in train and do not await Christ's return (2 Cor. iii. 18; iv. 4-6). It is characteristic of our writer that when it comes to 'strong' statements of man's relationship with God, much is left to the future End.

As before, the moral implications assert themselves, and what is in fact exhortation is put in the form of description of the Christian life. To hope for the promised outcome (seeing **him as he is**) means imitating his purity. While both **hope** and **pure** (*v.* 3) are new words in the Epistle,[1] the sinlessness of Jesus has already appeared in ii. 1 f. as that which qualifies him to be the sacrificial offering. So **pure** (*hagnos*) here is not without ritual overtones, as well as looking back to *dikaios* (**righteous**) in ii. 29 (cf. ii. 1). The man who hopes to **see him as he is** wishes to offer himself to God as a pure sacrifice. (In the phrase, **hope in him**, 'him' refers to Jesus.)

If we are right in suspecting that the idea of purity brings us within the sphere of the sacrificial rites of Judaism, then the transition to the next statement, which, though it is not on any showing an exact antithesis to *v.* 3, is partly so, becomes smoother. The link is the idea of observance or non-observance of the Law. The man who hopes for a blessed future keeps the law of purity. The man who sins, and so, implicitly, is without that hope, in effect breaks the law—for **sin is lawlessness** (*anomia*). The Old Testament admitted no distinction between the two words and used them in parallel: cf. Ps. xxxii. (LXX, xxxi.) 1 (quoted in Rom. iv. 7); Ps. 1, 4; Jer. xxxi. (LXX, xxxviii.) 34 (as quoted in Heb. x. 17). Our writer agrees, but finds it necessary to assert that the two concepts are identical, and that sin is to be thought of as law-breaking. However, 'the law' for him means above all (and perhaps exclusively) the command to love the brothers.

The fact that his mind moves in this direction, and, in the final clause, so deliberately, may indicate another facet of the writer's outlook and situation. For him, sin is not so much a cosmic force of evil, part of a philosophical-cum-mystical scheme, as a matter of rule-breaking, a matter for regulation by the discipline of the community, cf. i. 8 ff. and, for more detailed treatment, v. 16 f. Our writer is more concerned with 'sins'—despite the use of the singular in iii. 4 (contrast GJ i. 29; xvi. 8; though cf. xx. 23). He uses the plural in i. 9; ii. 2, 12; iii. 5; iv. 10; and it may be that even where the singular occurs, e.g. in i. 7 f., concrete acts rather than 'sin' in the abstract are in mind.

In v. 16 there is the comparable assertion (though the order is reversed) that **all wrongdoing** (*adikia*) **is sin**. 'Wrongdoing' like 'lawlessness' refers to acts which contravene established norms. There, the question being asked, implicitly, is: How may we

---

[1] The noun *elpis* (**hope**) occurs nowhere else in the Johannine writings and the corresponding verb never in a theological sense. **Pure** and **purify** also occur here alone.

define what comes under the heading of sin? And the answer is:
All wrongdoing. Here the question is: What is the character and
identifiable manifestation of sin? And the answer is: Acts which
break the law.

*V.* 4 then has a double purpose: it provides a partial antithesis
to *v.* 3, in that the sinner is contrasted with the man who has the
praiseworthy hope and aspires after purity; but it also seeks to
give concrete meaning to sin. That word is taken up in the following verse, where the thought turns back from the second coming
of Christ, which has been in mind from ii. 28 onwards, to the first
coming (revealing, cf. *v.* 2). Its purpose is expressed in terms
which recall i. 7 and ii. 2 (also GJ i. 29)—the removal of sins.
(In the earlier of those passages, it is worth noting, the reference
was to sins committed in the course of Christian life, here as in
ii. 2 it is to sins in general.) Christ was able to achieve this because
he himself was sinless (cf. above on ii. 3): once more the require-
ment of ritual sacrifice for a pure and unblemished victim is
probably in mind. How literally the writer takes his sacrificial
language it is hard to say; but within a few lines (iii. 8) he is able
to adopt a different, though perhaps not necessarily conflicting,
imagery—that of abolishing or undoing (NEB) the devil's works.

There are connections. The context is still at root eschatological,
and though here the reference is to what Christ's first appearance
has achieved, 'lawlessness' was a word not without apocalyptic
associations, with reference to the evil on the grand scale which
would reach its climax as the End drew near. And the devil or his
henchman (cf. iii. 8) had already been called in 2 Thess. ii. 3 'the
man of lawlessness'. In 1J, not only is there emphasis on the past
victory of Christ, but the devil himself is, as Bultmann says (Commentary, p. 55), 'historicized', seen concretely in the shape of the
heretics, the **antichrists** (ii. 18).

Before we leave these verses, there is another aspect of the
equating of sin with lawlessness. As with much else in this Epistle,
which at first sight is innocent of any such connection, it is probably part of the polemic against the heretics. They agree with their
opponents that lawlessness is blameworthy, but think themselves
free of it, just as they believe themselves to be sinless (i. 8). As
the one belief is illusory—they are in fact sinners—so is the other,
and no doubt specific acts could be indicated (cf. 3J 10).

A general statement follows, summing up the matter in familiar terms. Sinning and dwelling 'in Christ' are incompatible (cf. Philo, *de Fuga*, cxvii, 'as long as the holy Word is in the soul, it is incapable of sin'). But, as elsewhere, especially iii. 9 f., we face the question of consistency. How are these strong and unqualified assertions to be reconciled with the practical realism of i. 8 ff. and v. 16 f. (where the contrast with *v.* 18 is even more stark)? It is, we have seen, partly a matter of unresolved tension between two aspects of the writer's convictions: concerning the believers' status in relation to God and concerning the realities of moral performance and growth (cf. pp. 55 f.). The logic of his highly objective way of speaking of the Christians' status—as God's offspring— makes it hard to see how sin can now take place. But the facts speak otherwise, and demand a different kind of treatment.

Putting it in another way, it is a matter of aspiration as opposed to attainment. Now one, now the other, is in the forefront of the mind. Here, it is aspiration; but, as usual, it is stated in such a form that it reads like attainment. Even without the presence of factors as profound as the tension here between two forms of thought, such a dichotomy is not unparalleled in ordinary speech. The parent who says 'little boys do not do so-and-so' or the politician who affirms that 'Englishmen never behave in such-and-such a way' knows perfectly well that they do and that what appears as a statement of fact is in truth an expression of hope.

In our present passage, moral behaviour is the litmus test for the reality of status. If you sin, it proves that you are not within the circle of those admitted to the knowledge of the truth. Once more, we see how various expressions are for this writer simply alternatives: to **dwell in him** is clearly the same as to **know him** (*v.* 6). But is to 'see' him the same as to 'know' him? Almost certainly it is. To try to draw a distinction between two classes of Christians—eyewitnesses and the rest—is surely unreal. It is a question here of spiritual sight or perception (cf. p. 53): unlike i. 1, where the author ranges himself, as an orthodox believer, with, among others, the eyewitnesses who stood at the head of the tradition and whose testimony he shares.

**Let no one lead you astray** (*v.* 7): the use of this verb (cf. ii. 26), in another of the writer's brief, sharp injunctions, is the sign that the false teaching, to which the readers are dangerously exposed, is about to be countered. If this is the right way to take the passage, then we have here our clearest evidence that libertinism, or something approaching it, was one aspect of the heretics' creed. For them 'doing the right' is not *de rigueur*, not necessarily in their own estimate of themselves but certainly in the view of the writer and according to his canons of conduct. We should probably read the statement thus (*v.* 7): 'It is the man who does the right who alone can merit the epithet "righteous"—and that is not a description a Christian has any business to forswear because being righteous is a prime attribute of God.'

By neglecting the moral requirements of God, the heretics show where their antecedents really lie. They are children not of God (cf. iii. 1 f.) but of the devil. This accusation is levelled against the Jews in GJ viii. 44, when they do not—indeed cannot because of their diabolical parentage—'know' or 'hear' Christ's word. (In that passage, the devil is said to be a murderer: in 1J iii. 12, our writer refers to the case of the murderer Cain **who was born of the Evil One**.) The fact that heretical Christians can be spoken of in the same way may show that, in the writing of the Gospel, 'the Jews' were, partly at least, symbolic figures, standing for all opponents of Christ, including those of the writer's own day. It was a term whose application was capable of spreading, but only now does it denote opponents within the Christian circle itself. All have the same essential features, in particular that they spring from the devil and belong to him, apparently irredeemably.

In GJ viii. 44, the devil is said to have been a murderer 'from the beginning', as here he sins **from the beginning**. It is a case, like i. 1 and ii. 13 f., in which the word is used by our writer in its absolute, or virtually absolute, sense—the sense it nearly always bears in GJ (e.g. i. 1; vi. 64; but not in xv. 27 and xvi. 4)—not in its modified and 'ecclesiastical' sense, referring to the origins of the Christian movement or the life-time of Jesus (significantly, he never distinguishes the two), cf. ii. 7, 24; iii. 11; 2J 5 f.; see pp. 48 f. The devil is seen as a being who existed before the creation of the world and no doubt our writer knew stories of his fall from angelic status to begin his career as the arch-opponent of God's good purposes. **The beginning** refers to the moment of that mysterious, primeval disaster. It would be quite wrong to press questions which exercised later minds: was the devil coeternal with God? or was there something (what?) before 'the beginning'? and if so was this not a contradiction in terms, or could 'the beginning' be an event 'before' which there was God?

Another way of expressing the purpose of Christ's mission (in addition to saying that he came to remove sins, iii. 5) appears, as we have already seen, in *v.* 8: he came **to abolish the devil's works**. We may note the ethical, as distinct from, for example, revelatory, emphasis in both statements. The closely similar idea of the conquest of evil is applied to Christ in GJ xvi. 33, but in 1J, *tot verbis*, only to believers—the young men in ii. 13 f. and Christians in general in iv. 4; v. 4 f. More vividly, in GJ xii. 31 we see the Passion of Jesus as the moment when the devil ('the prince of this world') is cast out and when the climax of his 'works', the assault on the Son of God (GJ xiii. 2), is brought to nothing. It is likely that the death of Jesus is in mind in our present passage, though it is not explicitly mentioned: in this Epistle, specific references to the death of Jesus are relatively sparse and allusive (i. 7; ii. 2; iii. 16; v. 6 f.). His 'appearance' or 'being revealed', that is his coming to the world, is much more the chosen idiom of this writer. It accords oddly with his strong sense of the vital significance of the reality of Jesus' humanity (e.g. iv. 2), and indeed of his death (v. 6) that that death should receive so little attention; and perhaps it speaks for the correctness of our suggestion that this emphasis was not an integrated element in the writer's thought (cf. pp. 35 f.), but was rather something he felt obliged to defend against opponents even when his total outlook did not dictate it.

In *v.* 9 we have a variant on the formulation in *v.* 6, but this time in terms of parenthood. This idea was dropped after *v.* 2, then raised again in *v.* 8, with reference to the devil's offspring (that is, sinners in general but no doubt the heretics in particular). The writer reveals how simple the matter is for him: of course God's children do not and cannot sin—because, quite objectively, God's seed dwells in them.[1] (We may compare the similar expression concerning God's word in i. 10 and ii. 14.) We have not the

[1] We saw (pp. 88 f.) that the affiliations of the idea of rebirth are Hellenistic and Gnostic. The same is true of this aspect in particular. It is to be found in Corp. Herm. XIII, 2 (cf. p. 89), from almost two centuries after our present writing, and already in Philo, from some decades before. This Jewish writer, much influenced by Hellenistic thought of a kind that contributed to Gnosticism, could say of the people of Israel that 'their bodies were formed from human seeds, but their souls from divine' (*Life of Moses*, 1, 279). The elaborate scheme of Valentinus, the influential Gnostic of the second century, shortly after the writing of 1J, taught that those destined for salvation had the 'spiritual seed' implanted within them, thus ensuring their future.

slightest hint in this passage how this fact is to be reconciled with the sinfulness of those whom the writer still reckons within the orthodox community. In v. 16 f. he attempts a distinction between serious sins, for which no hope of forgiveness can be held out, and those less serious, for which intercession may be confidently made to God. However realistic this is as a way of attempting to deal with the problem and however reasonable it appears as an accommodation to the facts of life, it nevertheless deals a mortal blow to the doctrine enunciated here, as indeed does the pastorally less subtle treatment in i. 8 ff. (Note that in *v.* 6 the believer dwells in God, in *v.* 9 God's seed dwells in him. Either way of stating the condition for sinlessness is valid: the contradiction is formal only. Johannine teaching saw the indwelling of God/Christ and the believer as reciprocal, *v.* 24; iv. 12 f.; GJ xiv. 20; xvii. 21-3.)

*V.* 10 reveals the pressure which encourages the writer to adopt his clearcut doctrine. It must be made plain (cf. ii. 19) who are in the orthodox community and who are outside it. (The adjective **clear** is *phaneros*, related to the verb 'to reveal', *phaneroō*, and possibly giving off some of the same religious reverberations.) The two families, God's and the devil's, are to be distinguished by a clear test—that of conduct (cf. Matt. vii. 16, which may also be polemical—directed against antinomian Christians), in particular love of the brothers. We may suppose then, assuming that this last term is used in its common Johannine sense to refer to the true believers, that the fault of the heretics is twofold: they set more store by right belief (knowing what they consider to be the truth) than by right conduct; and they fail in the duty of love towards their Christian brothers, in effect the 'true' members of the congregation, who will be the recipients of the Epistle. The writer can formulate this test of membership of God's family because it is fundamental to the tradition they have received—as far as the Johannine church's tradition is concerned, it goes back to earliest days, to Jesus himself (GJ xiii. 34).

As Paul saw the membership of God's true people based on faith as no new principle, but one that carried their origin back to Abraham (Rom. iv. 1 ff.), so our writer (*v.* 12) sees the two families originating in Cain and righteous Abel, the latter murdered by his brother (Gen. iv. 8). Cain is therefore the very epitome of failure to obey the command of brotherly love. (For Cain as an example of wickedness, cf. Heb. xi. 4; Jude 11.) This

is the writer's only use of the Old Testament—a remarkable fact
in the work of one so Jewish in his affinities and so close to GJ,
which makes considerable use of it. It is not as if the Johannine
church sat lightly to the old scriptures. It is impossible to account
for this feature of 1J (and indeed of the other two Epistles). For
some reason, it must have seemed unpromising for the purposes
which led him to write. Perhaps argument based on Old Testament
passages would have been too easily open to refutation in a setting
and on a subject where Christian apologetic, at least in Johannine
circles, had not yet been developed. In GJ, a great many of the
Old Testament quotations, which are employed with great scribal
skill, are tools in anti-Jewish controversy (e.g. ii. 17; x. 34; xix. 36).
But by the time the Epistle was written, there was a new need:
polemic against dissident Christians, and for that the scriptural tools
had perhaps not yet been perfected, certainly they do not appear.
It is worth noting that the same observation, about the scarcity
of OT quotations and allusions, could be made about the
DSS.

**The world** (*v.* 13) is the sphere in which the devil's family
operates; so naturally, just as Cain hated Abel, it hates the
believers, cf. GJ xv. 18 f. This hatred contrasts with the love to
be found inside the community, the love which is seen as the
constitutive element of its existence. Love cements the community together. In this verse alone, where the writer consciously
draws the community together, he addresses them as his **brothers**,
identifying himself with them. Always elsewhere, they are his
dependants—'children' or 'dear ones', objects of his protection
or his love.

*V.* 14 is ambiguous: but the last clause depends on the verb
**know**, not on **passed**. So it does not mean that love brings about
the transition from the sphere of death to that of (eternal) life (cf.
i. 2; ii. 25; v. 11 ff.)—justification by works!—or even that the
conviction that the transition has taken place is only held because
brotherly love is observed to be present; but rather that the new
life is savoured and enjoyed, and its reality assured, in the atmosphere of love which prevails. **We know**: not in the sense of
intellectual demonstration but rather of experiential conviction.
The love shows the genuineness of God's gift to believers, not
because they are tempted to distrust it, but because they are concerned to show to those outside that this is their possession.

**Passed**, or 'crossed over' (NEB), *metabainō*, cf. GJ v. 24, where Jesus gives the assurance now seen to have been fulfilled.

If love is the sign of life, so hatred is the sign of death—the antithesis is once more completed. It is the sign of being outside the sphere in which eternal life is alone to be found. We may surmise that throughout this passage the reference is far from general, but that the heretics are very clearly in mind. It is they who not merely fail to put love first, but positively hate the brothers. Hatred is seen as, implicitly, murder, cf. Matt. v. 21 f.; and to take life is to forfeit any chance of possessing eternal life (*v.* 15). This is a sin for which intercession is of no avail; in terms of *v.* 16, it is **deadly sin**—literally 'sin towards death', sin which carries you into death's clutches (*v.* 14). Status and conduct go, as always, hand in hand. The man who belongs to the sphere of death brings about death. Such persons take life from others; Jesus, by contrast, gives his life for others (*v.* 16). And just as hatred, the lesser sin, is, implicitly, murder, so generosity is, implicitly, giving **our lives for the brothers** (see below).

It is noteworthy that until we come to v. 16, apart from the factual statement in ii. 19 that **they went out from us**, there is no hint of the possibility of movement from the one sphere to the other. It goes against our writer's scheme of belief to see the two as anything but fixed and determined. God has fixed the bounds. A man **dwells in death** (*v.* 14) or else has **life dwelling in him** (*v.* 15) (again, either kind of statement is acceptable, p. 97). Only at the end of his work does he openly contemplate the possibility that serious sinners can lose their hold on life: yet in the whole polemic against the heretics this is implicit. He prefers to hold, perhaps partly for the encouragement of his readers, that their apostasy is foreordained—they always belonged to 'the world' and 'the darkness', and it is natural that the truth would sooner or later become plain (cf. ii. 19).

'Love' needs to be expounded. Later, we shall learn that it is to be recognized fundamentally because it is God's essential nature (**God is love**, iv. 8), but now we find that it is defined by Christ's dying **for us**. His action shows the very meaning of the word. Moreover, it shows what the duty to love entails for his followers: they too must give their lives, not for others in general, but, as we should expect (cf. iii. 11 and GJ xiii. 34), for each other. (In GJ the expression—literally, 'to lay down one's life'—is used of Christ in x. 11, 15 and 17, of Peter, in bravado, in xiii. 37, and, as in our present passage, of the believer, in exposition of the meaning of love, in xv. 13.) **We know** is in the perfect tense, presumably because a past event, Christ's Passion, is in mind.

The sequel (v. 17) is surprising. Giving one's life immediately translates itself into the more manageable and less stringent duty of generosity to the needy brother. It seems that the one is even equivalent to the other. We have moved from crisis to daily living, and the shift may well be a revealing symptom of the setting to which 1J belongs, as compared with the Johannine Gospel. Not only is there no sign of crisis in which martyrdom is likely to be required (despite the fact that the End is believed to be near), but the essentially critical nature of the demand, as marked by the Cross, is softened, without comment or explanation, into an ethical programme. In GJ, though the injunction to love is so prominent, the ultimate nature of the Christian calling is never lost sight of: cf. xxi. 18. The centrality of the Cross is absolute, despite some theological tendencies which might have led away from it (e.g. the stress on Jesus as the revealer of heavenly truth). But here we are in the presence of Christian life which is settled and established, at least to the extent that virtue is esteemed most characteristically in the shape of kindness with material goods. Love of the brothers and giving one's life now find this quite concrete—and unheroic?—expression.

This transition from the demand for the giving of oneself to the demand for the steady giving of one's wealth and one's service (from the martyr to the monk) can be found elsewhere in the New Testament, for example in the change made by Luke (ix. 23) to the parallel in Mark (viii. 34): the demand to take up the cross loses all sense of crisis when it becomes a matter of daily, persistent discipleship. But nowhere else does it occur so abruptly within a single writer. It is as if he took up an existing piece of teaching—because it was current in his church—and immediately and automatically reinterpreted it along lines appropriate to his own circumstances. It is even possible that in using the expression ascribed to Jesus in GJ, he took it to mean not simply the Cross but Jesus' whole life of generosity, though he has perhaps sufficient sense of the centrality of Jesus' death to make this unlikely (cf. i. 7; ii. 2; v. 6 f.).

**Is wealthy**: literally, 'has this world's possessions' (*bios*, cf. ii.

16, p. 74). **Withholds his kindness**: literally, 'shuts up his bowels', that part of the body being seen at that time as the seat of warm, generous feelings. **Love of God**: that is, God's own love—which comes and dwells in the genuine believer (cf. ii. 5; iii. 1; iv. 10, 19), and is the source of the love in the believing community.

The need for love to find practical manifestation continues to be urged in *v.* 18. The˙distinction between lip-service and genuine virtue is reminiscent of the Epistle of James (i. 22; ii. 15 f.); cf. also Matt. vii. 21. Here and in Matthew, it may be a cut at 'heretics' of a speculative type, who, at least to the writer, were notorious as word-spinners ('intellectuals'—cf. the Gnostics of the next decades). In the case of James, it was aimed at Pauline Christians: which shows how impossible it is to give sense to the words 'orthodox' and 'heretical' at this time. In part, it is a charge which plain men always level at opponents, especially if other grounds of accusation are somewhat obscure!

**Genuinely** is literally 'in truth' and perhaps means no more than 'in real fact'; but probably it ought to have at least some of the stronger overtones of the word 'truth' in Johannine usage (cf. p. 66), though without echoing as far as its most developed sense, seen in GJ xiv. 6. (Cf. 2J 1 and 3J 1.)

We revert now (*vv.* 19 f.) to a question which came up momentarily in ii. 28. There we saw something of the writer's anxiety lest the Christians should lack **confidence** when they came before God on the day of Christ's return. How can they be certain that they will be secure on that day? In that passage the answer was that they were to **dwell in him**, and the sign of that was that they should do **what is right** (ii. 29). Now the same point is made more clearly. Here, **this** may be taken as referring back to the previous statement (despite the fact that in ii. 3, where the construction is the same, the word points to what follows). The meaning then is: if we are uncertain in our consciences whether we belong to the realm of truth, i.e. to God, then two converging lines of thought are there to reassure us. First, there is the objective test of moral behaviour—whether our love expresses itself in action. Second, there is the faith that God alone is the arbiter in this matter. He alone knows who belong to him, as he knows everything (cf. the believer's acquisition of this ability, ii. 27); and so he is in a position to **overrule** our doubts and give us the reassurance we seek. (**Assure ourselves**: literally, 'persuade our hearts', cf. Matt. xxviii. 14.)

The Greek is complex: in *v.* 20 *hoti* (**that**) is repeated unnecessarily: in our translation, which omits it, it would appear before **God**. This second *hoti* simply duplicates the first. Not surprisingly, it does not appear in some manuscripts, including the important Codex Alexandrinus (A). An alternative possible way of making sense, retaining both occurrences, is to turn the first *hoti* into *ho ti*, and translate: 'in whatever matter our hearts condemn us' (cf. Schnackenburg, Commentary, p. 202). The second *hoti* is then rendered 'because'.

Not only the theme of **confidence** but also the word (*parrēsia*) is picked up in *v.* 21, summing up the result of the preceding argument. **If our conscience is not against us** (or apparently, even if it is—for God overcomes our hesitations), we **approach God confidently** (lit. 'have confidence towards God'). The reference in these verses is not, as in ii. 28, to the Last Day, but to regular Christian life; and the purpose of Christian confidence is not to appear before God at the End, but in the present, in the act of intercession. Keeping **his commands** entitles us to undertake this task—to act as advocates before God in good causes, just as Christ acts as our advocate (*paraklētos*, ii. 1).

In GJ, this theme is expounded at greater length, and the same point is made: to be a member of the Christian body is to be assured of a favourable hearing at God's court. GJ xvi. 33 adds one element which is not expressed in 1J (but for the idea of **the name**, cf. *v.* 23); the asking is to be done in Christ's name, that is, on his authority and by virtue of one's relationships with him. The same assurance that faithful prayer will be heard and granted appears in Mark xi. 24 and James v. 16-18. It is both a fruit of virtuous life and a result of sharing in the life of the new age as the outcome of Christ's work. The Johannine passages reflect both considerations, the letter of James only the former.

The use of **commands**, plural, is unusual in the Johannine literature, though it is found again in ii. 3, 4; v. 2, 3; 2J 6; GJ xiv. 15, 21; and xv. 10. But there is no sign that these writers thought in terms of any other commands besides that of mutual love. Certainly, no other moral rules are stated, and indeed the single command appears less as moral guidance than as the expression of theological conviction about the Christian community and its life. We find here none of that taking over of the common ethical rules of the contemporary world, which is such a feature of, for example, the Pastoral Epistles, writings which reflect in many ways a situation comparable to that in our Epistles; nor do we find any awareness of a need to solve ethical problems or give detailed ethical advice. The question of the application of the command to love never comes in for treatment, except in *v.* 17, a case whose simplicity may be a sign of our writer's lack of interest in moral complexities.

The reference to keeping God's commands leads the writer to yet another statement of them—or rather of *it*. But despite the singular, which in *v.* 23 succeeds the plural of *v.* 22, the statement is twofold and in a new form. The command is both to believe and to practise: not just as elsewhere to **love each other**, but also to believe in the name of Christ. This is no doubt aimed at the heretics who err in both ways and separate the two (cf. ii. 3, 11). For this writer both are essential for the understanding of God's will. As for the order, we may compare *v.* 16, where again, acceptance of Christ comes first and leads to love.[1]

It seems at first sight strange to make belief a matter of command. Action may be required of a man but hardly belief. But the psychological difficulty which is so apparent to us did not strike this writer. His picture is of a God who rules the universe and may command as he pleases. It is his will that men should recognize his Son as his fully empowered and unique emissary (cf. ii. 22 f.), just as an earthly ruler may send his agent and order his subjects to accord him their recognition and loyalty. Nevertheless, **believe** in 1J does not just mean 'accept' but has something of a doctrinal character. It is partly 'trust', 'adhere to'; but it involves also belief in the truth concerning Jesus, cf. ii. 22; iv. 2, 14. The content of belief is both definite and crucial.

Morals and status are inextricably intertwined. To keep God's commands is to be linked with him in mutual indwelling. Though both God's dwelling in the believer (ii. 28) and the believer's dwelling in God (ii. 6, 24) have been mentioned, this is the first reference to the two together. In GJ, the reciprocal indwelling is always between Father and Son on the one hand, and Son and believer on the other, the Son acting as mediator, cf. GJ xiv. 20;

---

[1] This is the first use of *pisteuō* (**believe**). It occurs again in iv. 1, 16; v. 1, 5, 10, 13. The noun, *pistis*, is only in v. 4.

xvii. 21-3. The middle term is omitted here in 1J, as later in iv.
12 f., where the statement of iii. 24 is virtually repeated. The full
mediatorial role of Christ is taught much less rigorously in 1J than
in GJ (cf. p. 14).

The chapter finishes with the introduction of a quite new idea—
that of the Spirit. We know that God dwells in us, not now because
we keep his commands or because we love the brothers (iii. 14),
as we might expect, but because of the Spirit which he has given
to us. The next section will go on to explore what this means, and
if we are here at the seam between two originally distinct pieces,
then the introduction of this new theme is no doubt the editor's
work, to effect the join. At this point we may simply note once
more that whatever man has by way of relationship with God is
never the result of his own effort or initiative, but the gift of God.
So it was with the anointing (ii. 20), and the seed (iii. 9). Together
with Spirit, these make 1J's most concrete ways of speaking of
God's power and life coming to revitalize the heart of man.

## 6. THE TWO SPIRITS
### iv. 1-6

(1) My dear ones, do not trust every spirit, but test spirits to
see if they come from God: for so many false prophets have
been among those who have gone out into the world. (2) You
can tell the Spirit of God in this way: every spirit which
acknowledges that Jesus Christ has come in the flesh is from
God (3) and every spirit which does not acknowledge Jesus
is not from God. The latter is the spirit of Antichrist: you
have heard that he is coming and already he is in the world.
(4) You are from God, little ones, and you have overcome
them (i.e. the false prophets); because he who inspires you
is greater than he who inspires the world. (5) They belong
to the world; so they speak the world's language and the
world listens to them. (6) We belong to God. The man who
knows God listens to us, while the man who does not belong
to God does not listen to us. That is how we can tell the spirit
of truth from the spirit of error.

The impulse comes once more (as in ii. 18-27) from the threat provided by the heretics. The theme is again the duality which faces the Church: two ways of life, two spheres of existence, two families—and now two spirits. The passage revolves round words already familiar, **antichrist**, **world**, **overcome**, and **confess**; but **spirit** is added to the pattern.

In the remoter background there is the idea of God's spirit (Heb. *ruach* = breath, wind) as his powerful energy which could enable men to do what was normally beyond their power. This concept, of which we see ancient examples in passages like the stories of Gideon (Judges vi. 34) and of Samuel (1 Sam. x. 6, 10), was not obsolete, and could come to the surface in situations when religious fervour ran high. Such a situation was the launching of the Christian movement. So we find manifestations of abnormal, ecstatic behaviour in some of the early congregations (1 Cor. xiv). We find too, on the basis of a passage in the Book of Joel (ii. 28 ff.), a conviction that such manifestations are firm proof that the promised Last Day is on the brink of appearing, for such special divine activity would be one of its marks (cf. Acts ii. 1 ff.). However, instead of the belligerent behaviour which characterized spirit-activity in the heroic age portrayed in the Old Testament, the most common sign now was powerful speech (though cf. 1 Cor. xii–xiii for Paul's view of the full range of its manifestations)— whether unintelligible, in glossolalia, or intelligible, in inspired preaching. The Spirit of God enabled Christians to speak, whether in prayer to God (Rom. viii. 14 ff.), or in court (Mark xiii. 9 ff.), or in preaching and other Christian discourse (Acts ii; 1 Cor. ii; xiv).

There was, however, an awareness that it was not all plain sailing. There was a risk that not everything that seemed to flow from spirit-inspired utterance was genuine, or Christians might be led to despise and neglect it (1 Thess. v. 19 ff.). Or they might be led to resist another of the impulses of God's Spirit—towards moral life (Gal. v. 22; Eph. iv. 30, where again the close association of the Spirit with the Last Day appears). Our writer is particularly troubled—and it is the presence of heresy and schism which prompts him—by the question of criteria for telling when supposed spirit-activity was genuine. Here another element in the background becomes relevant.

In some Jewish circles, particularly those most influenced by the mythology of apocalyptic and by dualism of Persian provenance, the Spirit of God had been turned, rather more firmly than in other circles, into a distinct, quasi-personal entity—a hypostasis; and, to balance it, there had arisen the notion of another spirit—the spirit of error, or of iniquity. The evil principle came to be expressed in spirit-terms over against the good. In this sense, 'spirit' is a feature of the present, not only of the coming End.

We find this conception at Qumran. We read in the Community Rule (1QS iii. 18): '(God) has created man to govern the world, and has appointed for him two spirits in which to walk until the time of his visitation: the spirits of truth and falsehood. Those born of truth spring from a fountain of light, but those born of falsehood spring from a source of darkness' (Vermes, p. 75, cf. 1J ii. 9 ff.; iii. 1 ff.). The similarity with the doctrine of our present passage is striking. Once more, we realize what close relations the two writers are. Another comparable passage is in the somewhat later Testament of Judah (xx. 1): 'Know, therefore, my children, that two spirits wait upon man—the spirit of truth and the spirit of deceit. And in the midst is the spirit of understanding of the mind, to which it belongeth to turn whithersoever it will' (Charles, II, p. 322).

Corresponding to the two spheres of light and darkness, or truth and falsehood, and the two kinds of birth (of God and of the devil), the writer sees two spirits (iv. 6): **the spirit of truth** and **the spirit of error**. The former is the same as the Spirit of God (iii. 24); the latter's title (*planē*) is reminiscent of the verb 'to go astray' (*planaomai*), used of the heretics who are the agents of this spirit (ii. 26; iii. 7; cf. 2J 7). In these titles, the writer comes as close as anywhere in his work, as we have seen, to the terminology used at Qumran. It is interesting that in the Community Rule, 'works' seem to be the criterion for discriminating between spirits;[1] in 1J, it is belief, but iii. 24 redresses the balance.

According to the writer of 1J, Christians know that God dwells in them because he has given them a share in the Spirit. The implication is that this is a statement that can be verified. It is

---

[1] 1QS iii. f., Vermes, p. 76: 'It is (God) who created the spirits of Light and Darkness and founded every action upon them and established every deed upon their ways . . . These are their ways in the world for the enlightenment of the heart of man, and that all the paths of true righteousness may be made straight before him . . . : a spirit of humility, patience, abundant charity. . . . These are the counsels of the spirit to the sons of truth in this world.'

possible to point to aspects of Christian experience and life, and say: There you see the Spirit operating—that proves that God dwells in us. *V*. 2 tells what the criterion is: the acknowledgement that Jesus the Messiah came in the flesh. In the light of ii. 22 (p. 83), this means, we believe that Jesus—he and no other—came as 'Messiah-in-the-flesh'. If so, the view being refuted is that because Jesus was human, he could not have been wholly one with the Messiah, for man's 'saviour' must be a purely spiritual, quasi-angelic being (cf. pp. 35 f.). The verb (**has come**) is in the perfect, an emphatic statement of his appearance at a moment in the past.

On acknowledging Jesus (*homologeō*), cf. pp. 80 f. In *v*. 3, the expression is shorthand for not acknowledging 'that Jesus came in the flesh' (cf. *v*. 2). A variant is *luei*, i.e. 'annul (the truth of)'.

It is notable that the writer never says why it is a matter of such importance to his faith that Jesus came in the flesh. So much in his theology, in particular his depreciation of the world (e.g. ii. 15 ff.), would point to the type of teaching which we now find him attacking. His theology is not a wholly consistent pattern. It is derived from a variety of sources, and though it is true that in Judaism these disparate elements could already co-exist, it is not altogether easy to see how they could be held together. In this present case, it is probably anachronistic (though it is crucial in the Letter to the Hebrews) to see this emphasis on Jesus' real humanity as springing from a determination to see him as 'one of us'. That is not a major preoccupation at this time. Given our writer's thought elsewhere, it may be his sense of Jesus as a sacrifice for sin (ii. 2; iv. 10) which leads him to insist on this point. It may, however, be the fruit of his determination to hold fast to the fundamental Christian tradition. He is content to depart from some of the typical Johannine paths in the interests, it seems, of conformity with the ways of thought of other Christian groups. The manner in which the heretics have developed Johannine doctrine in the opposite direction has led to this reaction. We have already sensed it in the care to appeal to that which has been 'from the beginning' (e.g. i. 1; ii. 7; cf. pp. 48 f.).

But why is the idea of the Spirit associated with the confessing of the faith? It is partly to assert that true faith itself, like membership of the orthodox body, comes of God. But partly, in all probability, it is related to the occasion on which and the manner in which the acknowledgement of faith was made. It was uttered in the sublime, often ecstatic atmosphere of worship, and no doubt on the occasion of baptism. It was also spoken, though not necessarily in these present words (for they spring from points of controversy in the Johannine church), when Christians were arrested and ordered to answer for themselves in court (cf. Mark xiii. 11; possibly GJ xvi. 8 ff.). (This last situation does not seem to be in mind here.) In 1 Cor. xii. 3, we read of Paul's conviction that only the Spirit of God can enable a person to make the orthodox confession, there expressed as 'Jesus is Lord' (cf. Phil. ii. 11). In Ignatius' Letter to the Philadelphians vii (*ECW*, p. 113), there is a vivid glimpse of the inspiration by the Spirit of solemn utterance, this time by the leader of the congregation, addressing his people gathered for worship.

Paul gives an account of the process whereby the Spirit of God comes to occupy believers and to take over the role of reflection and reasoning hitherto undertaken, according to current psychology, by their own 'spirits'. His statement of the matter, in 1 Cor. ii. 10-16, is not unhelpful for the understanding of our present passage. 1J however works with the idea of a multiplicity of spirits (cf. 1 Cor. xii. 10). Here we have God's Spirit (singular), iii. 24, but there are also spirits (plural), which may—or may not—come from God. The same duality appears in the Revelation of John: compare ii. 7 etc. with i. 4, the reference to the seven spirits which are before God's throne. Neither there nor here is any difficulty felt in this two-fold expression. Spirits, or spiritual beings, were believed to exist in hierarchies and orders, dependent upon leaders and able to represent them in their activities in the world.[1]

The matter of identifying the Spirit of God (or of truth) was clearly both hazardous and urgent. Hazardous because believers were easily misled. They failed to keep their eyes on the foolproof test (iv. 2), and they were too readily impressed by the heretics' teaching, especially when presented in apparently inspired talk in an atmosphere of religious exaltation (cf. iii. 18). Urgent, as we can see from the fact that he no sooner mentions the Spirit than he warns of the need for care and discrimination: it is vital,

---

[1] In *v.* 3, **the latter is the spirit of Antichrist** is, literally: 'this is *the* of the Antichrist'. The italicized article is neuter and may mean (as we have taken it) that the neuter noun *pneuma* is understood, or it may mean 'this is the thing about Antichrist', or (NEB) 'this is what is meant by "Antichrist"'. There is also uncertainty over the text of this verse. Principally, some manuscripts amplify 'Jesus' by adding 'Christ' or 'Lord', a word otherwise absent from 1J.

in view of the approaching End, to keep the community pure and clear in its membership.

So it was essential to discriminate between authentic and false speech, and not enough to be moved by impressive exhibitions of religious feeling and conviction. Such speech or preaching was what was meant at this time by prophecy (*prophēteia*) (1 Cor. xii. 10; xiv); and it is plain that many groups in the early Church were exercised by the same difficulty which is here being exposed, that of distinguishing true prophecy from false. In 1 Cor. xiv, Paul had been chiefly concerned to make another distinction—between unintelligible speaking with tongues, of whose value he was sceptical, and intelligible prophecy. There the manner, here the content of the utterance, is chiefly in mind.

**False prophets** are attacked in Matt. vii. 15; xxiv. 11, 24, and we may compare the reference in 1J iv. 3 (cf. ii. 18) to the heretics, or their leaders, not indeed as 'false Messiahs' but as 'anti-Messiahs'. For another, more picturesque account of false prophets, see Didache xi–xiii, *ECW*, pp. 232 ff.

In various forms, then, the problem here discussed was widespread in the early Church. Nevertheless, the apparently general reference in iv. 1 is probably best taken as specifically relating to the heretics who here, as in ii. 19, are said to have 'gone out' (*v.* 1) —there **from us**, here **into the world** (cf. 2J 7)—leaving the sphere of light and truth, where alone true prophecy, inspired by God's Spirit, can be spoken.[1]

Spirits, like men, are **from God**—or else they are not (iv. 1, 3; cf. iii. 1, 9 f.); that is, they too belong to one of the two families, God's or the devil's. Spiritual beings and humans are all part of the same cosmos and hierarchy. It is important to grasp this aspect of the matter, if the writer's picture of the universe is to be understood. He looks out on a full and active universe which is all of a piece, ultimately, under its divine master, though in all its parts there is division and rebellion.

The orthodox believers are **from God** or God's offspring (*v.* 4), and this fact means that their victory over the false prophets is already as good as won: it is absolutely assured. The verb (**have overcome**) is in the perfect tense, cf. ii. 13, to be seen in the light

---

[1] *pisteuō*, in iv. 1, as in iii. 23, means 'acknowledge', 'trust', 'give faith to'. Bultmann (Commentary, p. 66) suggests: 'do not fall into the clutches of'. Spirits are powerful and seductive—they do not just wait passively to be recognized!

of GJ xvi. 33. **Them** must refer to the false prophets: it is widely separated from the noun (*v.* 1), but **Antichrist**, though singular, refers to the same people, and forms a bridge. The servants go by the master's name (cf. ii. 18, where the heretics are called **antichrists**).

The writer does not subscribe to a dualist system in which the universe is the battlefield of two essentially equally powerful spiritual forces. Rather, he knows that God (**he who inspires**, lit. 'is in', **you**) is stronger than the devil (**he who inspires**, lit. 'is in', **the world**). We might have expected 'them' rather than **the world**; but 'the world' is in the writer's mind as the place where the Antichrist is to be found (*v.* 3), and is very much his domain (*v.* 19). In any case, the false prophets belong to the world (in Johannine terms), so the shift is a minor one. (The translation we have used of the verb in *v.* 4*b* (also NEB) has the advantage of catching the context of ideas in this passage: the function of spirits is to inspire.)

**The world**, prominent in the writer's thought in ii. 15-17, appeared only three times in ch. iii (*vv.* 1, 13 and 17), but now it comes into fresh prominence, as the antithesis of the sphere of the Christian community where God's offspring live. In Johannine usage, 'world' is sometimes used in a neutral sense, from the point of view of evaluation—it is simply the sphere of man's life; and sometimes—more in 1J than in GJ—pejoratively. Here it is used in a 'worse' sense in *v.* 5 than in *v.* 3. From being a place it becomes a way of existence, a power that stands against God. (See p. 63 n.)

As we have found before, the frontier is regarded as clear and fixed. Membership of the two communities seems to be as good as predetermined, so that **the man who knows God listens to us, while the man who does not belong to God does not listen to us**. If those who know God are the existing members of the community, **us** must refer particularly to the leaders—primarily the writer, cf. i. 2. There is no clear sign of evangelistic concern in 1J; and this is of a piece with the Johannine negativity towards the outside world. The End is near, and the forces are aligned. It is almost as if our writer were prepared to abandon the world to his opponents, he has so little use for it.

The parallelism in the antithesis (*v.* 6*a*) is not complete, but the phrases are equivalents: to know God is the same as belonging to him or being a member of his family (literally, 'the man who is from God'), cf. *v.* 7.

The phrase 'from the world' (*ek tou kosmou*) is used in two senses in *v.* 5. (The literal translation is: 'They are from the world; therefore they speak from the world.') In the first case it signifies (like the parallel 'from God') the idea of possession or membership, as can be seen from a comparison with the use in iii. 9, iii. 10, iv. 7 or iv. 8. It may be seen as short for 'born from God'. But the second use in *v.* 5 means 'they speak as the world would have them speak'—at the world's prompting. As the Greek is linked, so NEB links the English of the two clauses: 'They are of that world, and so therefore is their teaching'—taking **speak** (*laleō*) in that specialized sense.

The phrase **spirit of truth** (though not its partner) occurs in GJ, where it is limited to the Supper Discourses, which look ahead to the life of the Church, in which the Spirit is at work, xiv. 17; xv. 26; xvi. 13; cf. also iv. 23 f. Despite this similarity, it is worth noticing that whereas in GJ, the terms Holy Spirit (e.g. xiv. 26; xx. 22) and *Paraklētos* are alternative expressions to 'spirit of truth', 1J prefers **the Spirit of God** (*v.* 2). Moreover, GJ prefers to link the coming Spirit more closely with Christ—it is a question of another Paraclete alongside Christ or in succession to him (xiv. 16; xvi. 14 f.); while in 1J, on the other hand, the Spirit centres on God. This is one aspect of a consistent tendency of 1J to be more theocentric and less christocentric in its doctrinal pattern than the Gospel. And it may be a further sign of 1J's lack of conceptual elaboration that the Gospel has no parallel to the rather concrete sense of the human manifestations of the Spirit's (and the spirits') activity found in the Epistle—though it may well lie only just below the surface in ch. xiv–xvi. From what we know of the life and the structure of the early Church, it is likely that the vehicle whereby the guidance of the Paraclete was conveyed was the leaders of the community—those whose 'spirits', in the slightly different terminology of 1J, will survive the testing which the writer counsels (cf. pp. 6 f.). Nevertheless, GJ does not speak of this openly, except perhaps in xx. 22.

# 7. THE MEANING OF LOVE
## iv. 7-21

(7) My dear ones, let us love each other, because love is from God, and everyone who loves is God's offspring and knows God. (8) He who does not love does not know God; because God is love. (9) God's love has been revealed to us by his sending his only Son into the world in order that through him we might live. (10) This is what love is: not that we have loved God, but that he loved us and sent his Son to be a sacrificial offering for our sins. (11) My dear ones, if God so loved us, we too ought to love each other. (12) No one has ever seen God. If we love each other, God dwells in us and his love is perfected in us. (13) We know that we dwell in him and he in us by the fact that he has imparted his Spirit to us. (14) And we have seen and we testify that the Father sent the Son as the saviour of the world. (15) Whoever affirms that Jesus is the Son of God has God dwelling in him, and he himself dwells in God. (16) We have come to know and believe the love which God has for us. God is love and he who dwells in love dwells in God, and God dwells in him. (17) This is the perfection of love among us, to have confidence in the day of Judgement; and we can have this confidence because even in this world we are as he is. (18) In love there is no place for fear; on the contrary, perfect love banishes fear, for fear has to do with torment. Anyone who fears has not reached the perfection of love. (19) We love because he loved us first. (20) If anyone says, I love God, and hates his brother, he is a liar; for the man who fails to love his brother whom he has seen cannot possibly love God whom he has not seen. (21) We have this command from him: he who loves God must also love his brother.

This passage consists almost wholly of statements which have appeared before. Because of this and because there is no clear connection of thought between *v.* 6 and *v.* 7, this section supports the view that behind 1J lies a set of Johannine pieces (homilies

may be the best classification), composed independently and so
naturally using in related but different ways much the same set of
ingredients. Some appear to be more closely related than others
to the present crisis in the Johannine church, and some may have
been adapted to meet the need.

The new section opens with a typical exhortation: **let us love
each other**; and the ethical injunction receives immediately an
equally typical doctrinal backing: **because love is from God,
and everyone who loves is God's offspring and knows God.**
Brotherly love is now the sign, not merely, as in ii. 28 and iii. 24,
of being born of God (though cf. iv. 7), but also of knowing him
(cf. ii. 3).

In *v.* 8, the doctrinal and ethical aspects of the writer's message
converge, and are welded into unity in the expression **God is
love,**[1] which is the summit of our writer's whole doctrine. The
moral concern which is so vital to his polemic is rooted in his
belief about God, so that it is impossible to receive the one without
the other. As Bultmann points out (Commentary, p. 71), what
we have in this phrase is not a theoretical or speculative definition
of God's being. It is rather a bold statement of the ground on
which the demand to love rests. So close are the ethical and
doctrinal aspects that throughout this passage the status conferred
issues in something very like infallibility of conscience.

But having attained his climax in thus epitomizing the character
of God, he moves down from the summit, first by loosening the
tight **God is love** to speak of **God's love**, and second by referring
to his other great datum of faith, the concrete expression of that
love in the coming of Christ. The assertion, **God is love**, is
immediately shown in its practical demonstration; man experiences
the love. Hitherto he has not spoken of that coming as springing
from God's love (though cf. GJ iii. 16), nor has he used the
Johannine word 'send' (*apostellō*, as here, or *pempō*), cf. also *vv.*
10, 14 (and GJ iii. 17; xvii. 3; xx. 21).

Love finds its definition—he reinforces his point—not in our
love for God (as, in his view, the heretics held), but in his love
for us. Our love for him can only be by way of response to his;
and his love is disclosed in the sending of his Son as the **offering for
our sins**. The word is that used in ii. 2 (*hilasmos*), cf. p. 62. Here,
it is associated with 'Son': possibly the story of the sacrifice of

[1] Cf. i. 5, **God is light**; and GJ iv. 24, 'God is spirit'.

Isaac, Abraham's specially designated son, is in mind. It was a
story much loved in Jewish piety and, though it was not yet prominent in Christian thought (but cf. Heb. xi. 17 and James ii. 21),
Paul (in Rom. viii. 32) alluded to it in speaking of Christ's death.[1]

We obtain eternal life **through him,** that is because of his love
for us. God is the source of love (cf. *v.* 19)—as he is the source of
salvation, for man's good is never self-generated. This fact, that
God is the source of love, is not simply a statement about the
universe. It carries with it a moral impulse: **if God so loved us,
we too ought to love each other** (*v.* 11).

The next clause (**no one has ever seen God,** cf. GJ i. 18) has
the air of being misplaced. It would fit very well before *v.* 20. But
there is no manuscript evidence for its belonging anywhere but
here. It is possible that it is an assertion against the wilder claims
of the heretics: they claim that their ecstatic spiritual experiences
bring them already even to the vision of God (cf. Schnackenburg,
Commentary, pp. 240 f.). (For our writer, less daring, the sight of
Christ is an object of hope when the End comes, iii. 2, cf. p. 91.)
But whether that be true or not, the point is in effect an abbrevi-
ated form of the argument in *v.* 20: we ought to love each other
as the proper manner of expressing our love for God, because it is
not possible to give direct practical effect to love for one who is
invisible. It is not uncharacteristic (cf. p. 14) that no attempt is
made to reproduce the strong christology which completes the
statement **no one has ever seen God** in GJ i. 18: 'the only
begotten Son (*monogenēs*, the same word as in 1J iv. 9), who is in
the Father's bosom, has disclosed him' (and cf. GJ xiv. 9). ('Only
begotten': unique in value and role, not only in fact.) The Epistle,
markedly more theocentric and less christocentric than the Gospel,
continues characteristically by speaking of God's dwelling in us
and of the perfecting of his love in us (cf. ii. 5). *V.* 13 harks back
to iii. 24, by expounding God's dwelling in us, to which he has
just referred, in terms of the gift of the Spirit which is its mark
and sign.

[1] A problem of translation and interpretation arises in *v.* 9. It is not clear
whether **to us** (literally, 'in us' or 'among us') refers to all in general—we may
compare the wide reference to the world in *v.* 14—or to the Christians in
particular. If the former, the translation ought to be 'among'. If the reference
is to the believers, it is possible that the phrase ought to be taken more closely
with **God's love,** which it immediately follows: 'the love of God in us was
revealed'.

Now, in *v.* 14, we have a statement about the Son which at first sight is very close to the second part of GJ i. 18. Is our writer then not 'higher' in his christology than we have given him credit for? For two reasons we decline to revise our original estimate. First, by contrast with the comparable statement in the Gospel, he does not say the Son is the one in whom the Father is revealed. Nor, for that matter, is there anything approaching the doctrine of GJ i. 14 concerning the 'becoming flesh' of the Word. Instead, the Father sends the Son to the world. He undertakes a task, rather than being the divine revealer. He is God's agent, not his very image. Secondly, the aspect of the mission of the Son which is noticed is that **we have seen and testify**. The point of interest is not the doctrine for the sake of its inherent truth—it is rather the task of propaganda and controversy to which the writer and those who stand with him are committed. In particular, that God truly sent Jesus into the world to save it (cf. iv. 2).

The two verbs echo i. 1 f. The writer places himself with the continuing and traditional witness of the Church. It is clear that **we have seen** does not refer to literal sight (as 3J 11 proves), for the object—**that the Father sent the Son as the saviour of the world**—is not open to the witness of the eyes. As elsewhere, the chief aim is to assert authenticity of belief and teaching. So there is no contradiction between the 'seeing' of *v.* 14 and the 'not seeing' of *v.* 12. The only sight of God which is possible and proper for man is that of the historical act of God in Jesus, and at the End that 'seeing' will be renewed, iii. 2. What is to be 'seen' of God is that he **sent the Son as the saviour of the world**. Just as in i. 1, there is some sheering away from the stronger affirmations of the Gospel: 'we have seen his glory' (i. 14); 'he who has seen me has seen the Father' (xiv. 9). Characteristically, the Epistle claims less for the *person* of Christ and prefers to draw attention to his work on God's behalf. It is a sign (which we have found before) of the less speculative, more 'orthodox' approach of this writer.

**Saviour of the world** occurs in the Johannine writings elsewhere only in GJ iv. 42, but the idea is present in GJ iii. 17; iv. 22; cf. 1J ii. 2. The frequency of 'saviour' (*sōtēr*) as a title for Jesus in more recent Christian parlance is not supported by the witness of the New Testament writers. In the undoubted Pauline writings it appears only once (Phil. iii. 20). The word appears three times in 1 Timothy, but always with reference to God (as also in Luke i. 47); though in the other Pastoral Epistles it designates Jesus (2 Tim. i. 10; Titus i. 4; ii. 13; iii. 6; but contrast Titus i. 3 and iii. 4). It is used for Jesus five times in the Second Epistle of Peter, but once for God in the related Epistle of Jude. The evidence indicates, then, that in so far as early Christians made use of the term, they were as likely to apply it to God—as the Old Testament had done (e.g. LXX of Deut. xxxii. 15; Isaiah xii. 2; xvii. 10; xlv. 21 f.)— as to Jesus, and it only becomes at all common in the later years covered by the writings of the New Testament. Common in the religious aspiration of the Hellenistic world, it did not commend itself to the Christians as a leading title for their Lord. The related noun, 'salvation', is much more common, especially in the writings of Paul.

The phrase as a whole raises a question. It is not at first sight clear how such a statement is to be reconciled with the writer's generally negative attitude to the world (cf. p. 63 n.). How serious in his view is the enterprise of the world's salvation? Is it from the start a forlorn hope? Certainly 1J has no worked out conception of a mission to the world. It is hard to resist the judgement of Käsemann (*The Testament of Jesus*, London, 1968), based chiefly on GJ, that for John 'the world is the object of mission only in so far as it is necessary to gather the elect' (p. 65).

The terms of the affirmation in *v.* 15 differ from those of ii. 22 and still more of iv. 2. **Son of God** may have had some currency in Judaism as a title for the Messiah, in which case this verse is simply equivalent to ii. 22, but there is no mention here of 'the flesh'. The point must be that the heretics believed perfectly well in the Son of God but refused to identify him with the human Jesus (cf. pp. 34 f.). He was in their eyes a spiritual being who had joined himself with Jesus temporarily but was essentially of the other world, immune from the attachments of the flesh, with the suffering and death that accompany it. For the expression of the mutual indwelling of God and the believer contained in this verse, cf. iii. 24.

What does it mean to **believe the love** (*v.* 16)? Presumably the sense is that we believe that God's love is bestowed on us, or that we have confidence in this love. The other sense of the verb *pisteuō* ('trust') is not far away. The rest of the verse simply repeats *v.* 8, and unfolds its implications in relation to the idea of mutual indwelling. If **God is love**, then to dwell in him is to dwell in love.

The sign of perfect love (i.e. the love of God in us, cf. ii. 5; iv. 12) will be that we come before him confidently at the Judgement (cf. ii. 28; iii. 21).

The causal clause which now follows is difficult. Why should it be that the reason for our having confidence on the day of Judgement is that **even in this world we are as he is**? And what precisely is the point of comparison between 'him' and 'us'?

We need first to establish the identity of the **he** (*ekeinos*). The immediate context makes it most natural to refer the pronoun to God (*v.* 16); but the fact that all other uses of *ekeinos* in 1J (ii. 6; iii. 3, 5, 7, 16; v. 16 is not relevant) refer to Jesus, and the closeness of the likeness envisaged between 'him' and the believer, reminding us of iii. 2, make it almost certain that the reference is to him.

Though there is a resemblance to iii. 2, the point now is precisely what the earlier verse does not say. There the Christians' present status as God's children is accepted as imperfect: **what we shall be has not yet been revealed**. More is in store at the End—and only then shall we **be like him, because we shall see him as he is**. It is then strange that in the present passage this likeness is affirmed to exist already **in this world**; all the more so because the sentence is about the future day of Judgement. The conviction expressed in iii. 2 could reasonably have been repeated here. This seems no place to speak of our future **in this world**.

Moreover, what is the force of **as he is**? If the reference is to the present, heavenly life of Christ, then this is the only place in 1J where it is mentioned, apart from ii. 1, and there it concerns the specific matter of his being our advocate before God when we sin. And how can Christ's present state be related to our fate on Judgement day? Both his past (as example) and his future (as defender and supporter) would be understandable—but this is not! Further, it may fairly be read in such a way that **in this world** refers to Christ as well as to us, thus making the confusion complete.

It is not surprising that scribes found themselves altering the text at this point. Some minuscule manuscripts replaced 'as he is so we are' (to use a literal translation which makes the comparison clearer) by 'as he was spotless and clean in this world, so we too shall be', thus comparing Jesus' past with our future and firmly moralizing the passage. And the excellent uncial manuscript Codex Sinaiticus replaced **we are** by 'we shall be'.

Bultmann (Commentary, p. 77) is sure that the text is severely dislocated and puts forward without much assurance a more radical hypothesis for the reconstruction of the original. The passage is full of confusions. Whereas in ii. 28 the confidence referred to is that which Christians are to have before Christ at his return, here, in the text as it stands, it must be confidence before God, because he presides at the Judgement (cf. iii. 21; v. 14, where again the word is used of confidence in relation to God, though in both cases in the present life). This only adds to the difficulty, for *ekeinos* virtually has to refer to Christ (see above), and the shift in reference is too abrupt; and if, as is most unlikely, *ekeinos* here did refer to God, it is not clear what the point of the comparison could be. Finally, if the **confidence** were able to be taken as confidence before Christ rather than God, then the phrase **as he is** would make no obvious sense. Taking a hint from GJ xv. 10, Bultmann suggests that the original comparison concerned Christ's and our being in the Father's love. The phrase **in this world** stood after **to have confidence**, whose reference was then to this present life as in iii. 21 and v. 14. The statement that **in love there is no place for fear** then followed naturally (cf. Seneca, *Ep.* xlvii. 18, *non potest amor cum timore misceri*, 'love cannot be mixed with fear', Loeb edition, 1953). The phrase **on the day of Judgement** is, like other apocalyptic references according to Bultmann, an intrusion by the 'ecclesiastical' reviser (cf. p. 27) into a passage which was originally about the Christians' present life in relation to God. A literal translation of the verse, as conjectured, then runs:

'By this has love been perfected among (with) us, that we may have confidence in this world, because as he is in the Father's love, so also are we in his love.'

However, perhaps the text as it stands, though undeniably obscure and imprecise, need not be abandoned as meaningless. Admittedly, the transition from the future (**the day of Judgement**) to the circumstances of the present is abrupt, and there is some inconsistency with iii. 2.[1] But it is doubtful whether this is more

---

[1] An inconsistency which, unless we accept his highly conjectural importation from GJ xv. 10, Bultmann's suggestion of eliminating the future reference does nothing to relieve.

than the kind of change of emphasis or standpoint which occurs throughout 1J. Sometimes, in controverting the heretics who lay too much store by the perfection of the status they have already achieved, he has to point to what remains to be done; iii. 2 is one example, and another is the discussion of the constant need for sins to be forgiven, i. 8–ii. 2. But elsewhere he writes as if for him too the gift is already assured and complete, e.g. iii. 9, 24; iv. 4. Indeed this emphasis is stronger than the other.

So it is by no means surprising that he can base confidence for the future day of Judgement on a status already conferred. (Passages like Matt. x. 32 and Luke xii. 8 throw some light; there too the present will avail for the believer on the coming Day.) In that case, **in this world** must refer only to the believers, not to Christ: they are now already on earth as Christ is in heaven. The doctrine, if not the expression of it, is fully Johannine—more so, as far as this aspect is concerned, than almost any other passage in 1J. Indeed, it may be just because the doctrine of mutual inter-action between Christ and the believer is so underdeveloped in this writing that when it is expressed, the statement of it is so inco-herent. It is less than immediately congenial to the writer of the Epistle. But if GJ xvii is read as a statement of the relationship between the exalted Christ and his followers on earth, then 1J iv. 17 presents few difficulties as a succinct reference to the same essential teaching.

It may be that the feature of Christ's present existence which is particularly in mind is *his* perfect confidence before God—he is wholly qualified to be our advocate (ii. 1), the one sure of a hearing. So we have confidence now as well as at the Judgement. If this interpretation is right, then it is wholly natural that the idea of fear should immediately be raised. We have a boldness like his.

**Fear** (*v.* 18) is the antithesis of confidence. Therefore, as God's love with us provides our confidence, fear is excluded—that is, fear of God or in relation to God. When God's love fills us com-pletely (*v.* 17; cf. ii. 5), then fear is wholly cast out. If a man is afraid in the presence of God, it is a sign that God's love does not fill him (there is 'space' for this quite contrary disposition), and so that he belongs to 'the other side'. Therefore—the thought is still of the future Judgement—the torment that awaits those cut off from God is in store for him. But (*v.* 19), the believers are fortunate because God's love has filled them—and once more, the essential divine initiative is made plain: **we love because he loved us first**. With this statement, we may compare the following, from the contemporaneous Jewish composition, the Odes of Solomon (iii. 3): 'For I should not have known how to love the Lord, if he had not continuously loved me' (see Charlesworth, op. cit., pp. 107 ff., especially p. 128).

And immediately, we find too the vital moral demonstration, *vv.* 19 ff. (cf. iii. 16 ff.), as the theme of brotherly love is resumed, after the interruption of *vv.* 13–18. To fail in this test is to show that one is a liar—not simply being deliberately untruthful in speech, but proving that one does not belong to the sphere of truth (cf. i. 6, p. 66).[1]

One other question is raised by *v.* 19. Who is the object of the verb **we love**? Is it God or one another? The balance of the sentence as a whole demands the former: our love for God returns his for us. So does the argument of the succeeding verses, concerned to show how the genuineness of love for God may be tested. This passage then complements *vv.* 10 f., where the same starting-point (that God's love is prior to ours) issues in the other line of thought—that God's love for us must lead us to love each other. This is surely the correct interpretation, despite a tendency to follow in this verse the lead of the formidable array of previous statements where the object of our love is clearly 'each other' (iii. 14, 18, 23; iv. 7, 11).

The statement of Christ's (or God's)[2] command (*v.* 21) recalls the dual command, to love God and the neighbour, found in the Synoptic Gospels (Mark xii. 28–34 and parallels). This passage can be seen as an attempt to explore the relationship between its two parts. But here, as always in the Johannine writings, **brother** replaces 'neighbour', and we have no reason to believe that the **brother** of this formulation or of iii. 17 represents any wider circle than **each other** in passages like iii. 11, 23; iv. 7, 11, 12; cf.

---

[1] It is not clear whether the first verb in *v.* 19 is in the indicative (as in our translation, **we love**) or the imperative, 'let us love'. We are on the whole led to the former by iv. 8–12 and iv. 20–v. 2, though iii. 18 and iv. 7 point firmly in the other direction. On the basis of the context the indicative is to be preferred, and the presence in the Greek of the two pronominal subjects (*we* and *he*) confirms this view.

[2] The text says ambiguously: **We have this command from him.** The subsequent clause makes it likely that **him** refers to Christ, and NEB is bold enough to put this into the text. In fact, a number of significant manuscripts took the other view, reading 'from God'.

2J 5; GJ xiii. 34. As we have seen, the Johannine church is conscious of itself as the enclosed community of the redeemed, and
love is the cohesive moral force of its common life. This is the
situation in the Gospel, portrayed above all in the Last Discourses,
with their private setting, shut off from the outside world, in the
room of the supper. In 1J it is reinforced by the existence of
schismatic and heretical members: a conspicuous element in the
charge against them is their failure, from our writer's point of
view (would they have said the same to him?), to preserve this
cohesive bond.[1]

## 8. WITNESS AND FAITH
### v. 1–12

(1) Everyone who believes that Jesus is the Messiah is God's
offspring, and to love the parent means to love the child;
(2) and we know that we love God's children if we love God
and carry out his commands. (3) For to love God means to
keep his commands; and these commands are not burdensome, (4) because every child of God overcomes the world.
It is our faith which has overcome the world. (5) Who else
overcomes the world but the man who believes that Jesus
is the Son of God? (6) He—Jesus Christ—came by water and
blood, not water alone, but water and blood. The Spirit is
the witness to this, for the Spirit is truth. (7) In fact there are
three witnesses, (8) the Spirit, the water and the blood, and
the three are one. (9) If we are willing to receive human
testimony, we should certainly accept the stronger testimony
of God; for this testimony is indeed that of God—it is the
witness he has borne to his Son. (10) He who puts his trust
in the Son of God has this testimony in himself. He who has
no faith in God has made him out to be a liar, because he
has not accepted the testimony which God has borne concerning his Son. (11) The testimony is this: God has given

---

[1] For a possible parallel in the Dead Sea Scrolls to the sequence of argument
in these verses, see Charlesworth, op. cit., p. 160. At Qumran, the term was
'neighbour', but it meant the fellow-member of the community, just as in the
underlying text, Lev. xix. 18, it referred to the fellow-Jew.

**us eternal life and this life is in his Son. (12) He who has the Son has life; he who does not possess the Son of God is without life.**

This section centres on the nature and content of faith, just as the last section argued out the rationale of the obligation to love. In fact, the boundary between the two sections is blurred: it may be that the first four verses should go with the earlier piece (as Bultmann and Schnackenburg suggest in their commentaries)—the first three verses clearly maintain the theme of love; or it may be that, if we have in this Epistle a collection of originally independent compositions, these verses are a bridge made by the editor between one section and another. Once more we find only one or two substantially new ideas, but as before the old ideas revolve around a fresh centre, this time faith and the witness that is borne to it. Five out of nine occurrences of the verb *pisteuō* (believe or trust) occur in these verses (and one of the remaining four is in *v.* 13), and the only use of the noun, which never occurs in GJ, is in *v.* 4.

Still, new Johannine words are often close to old ones in sense. So though *pisteuō* is new, it is not very far from *homologeō* (acknowledge or confess, cf. ii. 22 f. and iv. 2), especially as it carries a mixed sense of 'believe' and 'trust', and signifies active affirmation, not passive acceptance. The core of the orthodox faith, with which the passage opens, is expressed as it was in ii. 22: that **Jesus is the Messiah**. In effect, the meaning is the same as the earlier statement of the content of faith in iii. 23: **to believe in the name of his Son, Jesus Christ** (i.e. Jesus Messiah, with the title probably still retaining its proper sense, and not being simply part of a personal name). To believe in the name of Jesus Christ is to believe in his true nature and role. In that passage too (as in *v.* 1*b*), this belief is immediately associated with love for the brothers—though here there is a middle term: love for God.

In what sense does holding this faith signify that one is **God's offspring**? It is not that the act of belief brings about the status —as it were, ensures adoption by God (as in Paul's thought, Rom. viii. 15, 23; Gal. iv. 5); rather, that making the affirmation shows that one belongs to the family of God and not of the devil (just as in iv. 7 f. brotherly love has the same function). The thought is in principle deterministic, though it is by no means fully expressed: it is simply assumed that the two spheres—and their membership—are 'given'.

In that case, the connection between the two halves of the statement in *v.* 1*a* is not of the same kind as the connection in *v.* 1*b*. In the latter, it is not that loving the parent shows that you love the child; rather, loving the parent carries with it an obligation to love the child. In our translation, we have taken this as an illustration; 'the begetter' and 'the begotten' are general terms. But even if this is right, the illustration leads the reader immediately to that which it illustrates; and perhaps we should see instead a reference to God, the Father, and either Jesus as his Son or the believer as his child, an interpretation which certainly makes the argument more direct. If **the child** means Jesus, then the reference to him in *v.* 1*a* can be seen as looking on to the second half of the verse and the linking of the two halves by **and** is wholly natural. Otherwise it is not easy to see any close connection of thought. But in *v.* 2 we read of our love for **God's children** as well as for God himself, and *v.* 1*b* may reasonably be taken as already introducing these two aspects of love. In that case, the link between the two halves of *v.* 1 can only be that the faith there stated and the status which accompanies it express themselves in the twofold love for God and the fellow-Christian.

*V.* 2 also lacks lucidity. The usual teaching of the work (cf. iii. 14, 18 f., and possibly v. 1) is that the proof of Christian status (whether seen as membership of God's family or in terms of being 'of the truth', iii. 19) lies in obedience to the command to love the brothers. Here, however, the sign that we love our fellow-Christians is that **we love God and carry out his commands**; and we know (it is the Johannine doctrine) that those commands amount simply to loving the fellow-Christians (cf. pp. 102 f.). The argument is then circular. And it is not easy to see how loving God helps us to **know** that we love our Christian brothers, as distinct from, for example, 'feeling impelled' to love them (the argument of *v.* 1): unless the intention is to show that each kind of love is the demonstration of the genuineness of the other, each reinforcing the other. In that way the circularity may be justified at the bar of practical experience.

As usual, each statement gives rise to the next, without much regard for a complete line of argument. So mention of our love for God leads to the explicit definition of that love in terms of obeying his commands, *v.* 3. Literally: 'this is the love of God, that we keep his commands'; 'love of God' must, in view of *v.* 2 *b*, mean our love for God, not his for us. **These commands are not burdensome**—for the quite objective reason that the Christian has power to conquer **the world**, whose lure and strength would otherwise make them so. The idea has appeared already, ii. 13, where the young men of the congregation are said to have conquered the Evil One. We saw how the writer thinks of this objective power in iii. 24–iv. 6, where he speaks of the Spirit (p. 105). The Spirit is the force which impels the Christians towards their victory and assures them of it.

The verb is in the present—**overcomes**. Does it mean that the Christian—the child of God—either performs or should perform actions which can be described as the conquest of the world? Or that the very fact of being a member of God's family means that one is in the community in which that victory is effective and the world's power is shut out? The statement that the **commands are not burdensome** implies that the latter sense is intended. One's membership of God's family is itself a source of strength which enables one to keep the commands and so to 'overcome evil with good' (Rom. xii. 21). The conquest goes on continually.

We may contrast Jesus' triumphant assertion concerning his Passion: 'I have conquered the world' (GJ xvi. 33). That sense of Christ's victory, achieved once and for all, has now been transmuted into the constant battle of the Christian life. The eschatological has given place to the ethical. From iv. 4, we can see that the overcoming of evil has one very concrete manifestation— the defeat of the heretics. It is the only specific example that is given. And according to that verse, with its optimistic (we may suppose) use of the perfect tense, this aspect of the victory was already complete. The writer has no doubt of the power at his disposal. There, the reason given for their victory is that God, with his superior power, is 'in' them, that is, he gives them his own power with which to fight. Here, it is the fact that they are God's offspring.

The second half of *v.* 4 means, literally: 'this is the conquest that conquers the world, our faith'—that is: 'Our faith enables us to overcome the world.' It acts as a weapon of war, and its force consists in the fact that its content is the true nature of Jesus. He is the Son of God (cf. iv. 15, p. 116), that is the full and effective

agent of God. Strictly, it is not the belief itself that conquers, but
the believer. To that extent, *v.* 5 restates *v.* 4 *b*, and makes it more
concrete.

Jesus the Messiah (the title may well be used deliberately, following from the dogmatic definition of *v.* 5) is defined as the one who
**came by water and blood**. To us the words are enigmatic, but
in their original intention they must have been both clear and
concrete in their application. They are designed to give firm
content to the belief that Jesus is the Son of God. We have
suggested earlier (p. 116) that this title was common ground
between the writer and the heretics, signifying the saviour or
Messiah whom both revered. Where they differed was on the
matter of identifying this figure fully with the earthly Jesus, both
in his life and his death. In other words, the issue is the same as
that raised in iv. 2: Is Jesus the Messiah-come-in-the-flesh? In our
present passage, the words **water** and **blood** somehow serve to
pinpoint this crucial identification. How do they do it?

The reader who comes to 1J with a knowledge of the Gospel of
John will begin by thinking that both terms focus attention on
Jesus' death. The reference is to the effusion of water and blood
from the side of Jesus at the time of his death (GJ xix. 34), and
the purpose is to demonstrate the physical reality of his death.
There was no evasion of all that goes with existence in the flesh.

However, it is not clear that this is necessarily the point being
made in the Gospel passage. It is possible that a different doctrinal
significance is intended; the point is perhaps that the two sacraments of baptism and eucharist derive their meaning and validity
from Jesus' death (a point already made by Paul, Rom. vi. 3 ff.;
1 Cor. x. 16; xi. 26). If the verb (**came**) had been in the present,
this might easily have been the sense; but it renders an aorist
participle and can hardly refer to anything other than a single past
(rather than a repeated) event. Or the intention may be the simpler
one of impressing upon readers the wonder of the happening at
Jesus' death and the strength of the testimony borne to it (cf. GJ
xix. 35).

But these interpretations, based on a supposed link with the
Gospel incident, founder on the phrase, **not water alone, but
water and blood**. In the passage in the Gospel, the two belong
together inseparably, and we must seek a meaning for them in
which they could plausibly be distinguished. The heretics, it

seems, find it harder to accept whatever is meant by blood than whatever is meant by water.

If we are right in supposing that the general purpose is to assert the genuineness of Jesus' human existence, then their most likely reference is to his baptism and death, the termini of his earthly career. The heretics believed that the redeemer was involved in the baptism of Jesus, but not that he was involved in his death. This accords with the known views of early Gnostic teachers, such as Cerinthus, and we are therefore fortified in adopting this exegesis. The heretics believed that the divine, spiritual redeemer entered the man Jesus at the moment of his baptism, but, being impassible and belonging to the realm of immunity from death, he departed from him before the crucifixion.

A difficulty with this largely convincing view is that the Johannine account of Jesus' life does not mention his baptism. GJ recounts the meeting between John the Baptist and Jesus (i. 29 ff.) but has no reference to the baptism which in the other Gospels occurs at this point. If the writer of GJ knew any of the other Gospels or even what must have been common tradition about Jesus, then we must think of this as a deliberate omission and try to find a reason for it. The same difficulty occurs in relation to the Last Supper. Again, the framework of the occasion is there, but the incident itself is not described. In both cases, this may be partly because the stories were well known from other accounts, and partly because their significance is conveyed in other ways (the descent of the Spirit in i. 32 gives the commissioning of Jesus and the discourse on the bread in ch. vi has the evangelist's teaching on the eucharist). But there may be a further motive in the present case. The story of Jesus' baptism raised difficulties, for it told of the sinless Lord subjecting himself to a rite concerned with the removal of sin. The words inserted by Matthew in the Markan story of the baptism of Jesus are almost certainly an attempt to answer a question along these lines (Matt. iii. 14 f.); and Luke is probably responding to the same pressure when he passes hurriedly over this aspect of the encounter between the Baptist and Jesus, relegating it in his telling of it to a genitive absolute (Luke iii. 21). As GJ takes the process a stage further, omitting all mention of such an act, it is somewhat surprising that 1J can rest an important argument on a reference to it. But perhaps this view of the Johannine omission is mistaken, or perhaps the

Johannine church (and indeed the heretics, for they too accept **the water**) has now ceased to feel the difficulty with the baptism story, possibly in the light of the factors which, we believe, have led to its being brought to prominence here: that is, its importance is now seen as binding 'the Messiah' to Jesus the man—as far as the orthodox are concerned, to the point of identity.

In iv. 2, the word selected to make the required point was 'flesh'. Here, 'water' and 'blood'. If for the moment, we may count GJ's story of the encounter between John the Baptist and Jesus as, even if by default, a baptism story, then these two terms stand for the beginning and end of Jesus' ministry and enclose the rest—'the flesh'—between them. The Gospels of both Mark and John (especially the former, with its absence of resurrection stories) cover precisely this span, as far as Jesus' earthly life is concerned. **Blood** points to Jesus' death as a sacrificial offering, cf. i. 7; ii. 2; GJ xix. 34.

The authenticity of this faith in Jesus, who truly lived and died as the Messiah, is attested by the Spirit—that is, the Spirit of God (iv. 2) or of truth (iv. 6). (Here, **the Spirit is truth**, that is, it belongs to the sphere of truth and what it inspires is genuine and trustworthy.) How does the Spirit testify to these things? In the inspired utterances which are to be heard in the meetings of the church—so we may suppose (cf. pp. 6 f.). In these solemn and impressive statements, the true faith is spoken. They are so clearly authentic that the seal is firmly placed upon the teaching they contain.[1]

The two references to water and blood in *v.* 6 differ, in that there is no article before the nouns in the first case, whereas in the second it appears. The difference may be deliberate. Jesus came by means of these two elements, that is they were the instruments of his real humanity. But this water and this blood were specific instances of the elements—the water of his baptism and the blood shed at his death.

In *v.* 7 a difficulty is immediately apparent. Whereas we have just seen the Spirit as the witness to the role of water and blood,

---

[1] Some manuscripts, including the important codices Sinaiticus and Alexandrinus, add 'and spirit' after **blood** in *v.* 6 *a*, in order to harmonize with *v.* 7. Others, less significant, replace **blood** with 'spirit', no doubt to bring the passage into line with GJ iii. 5. The first variant is in line with the fascination exerted upon the Patristic mind by the triple witness, issuing above all in the famous comma in *vv.* 7 f., cf. p. 42.

now all three appear together as witnesses. In accordance with the rabbinic criterion for solid truth, the three agree (cf. Deut. xvii. 6; xix. 15; Matt. xviii. 16; Heb. x. 28). But can water and blood mean the same here as in the previous verse, now that their role is quite different? Most commentators believe that they cannot. But then disagreement arises: was *v.* 7 inserted into the text, either by the final redactor, or at some later stage (like the comma which came later still, cf. p. 42)? Or is this an instance of the Johannine capacity for making symbols bear more than one sense? The Epistle is in any case not notable for sticking to the strict path of tightly ordered thought.

Clearly the reference in *v.* 7 is to three realities of the Christian life. The Spirit occupies that role in *v.* 6, giving the faith in the historical Jesus power in the present; and now the Spirit is joined by **the water and the blood**: the three are spoken of together, and they agree in their testimony. All three testify to the reality of Christian existence. But to what do the three terms refer?

The element in Church life denoted by the Spirit is most likely to be still what it was in *v.* 6—that is, authoritative and impressive verbal statement. If we ask what other elements, which could plausibly be designated 'water' and 'blood', may fit alongside such statement and reinforce its testimony, then baptism and eucharist are the best candidates. We may even envisage the concrete circumstances in which such an association would arise—though admittedly there is no word in 1J to support the conjecture. It was, we suggest, the gathering of the church for worship, in which both inspired preaching and the administration of baptism and eucharist took place, under the presidency of the community's leaders.

Such an interpretation leads us back, as far as *v.* 7 is concerned, towards a meaning for **blood** and **water** which we were inclined to reject in *v.* 6. We have already said that a shift would not be uncharacteristic; in any case, the two senses are not so far removed from each other. The baptism of Christians was probably seen as partly an imitation of the Lord's own baptism, and the story of the latter may already have been influenced by the rite for the former. Matthew's explanation of the baptism of Jesus as 'to fulfil all righteousness' (iii. 15) may well mean that Jesus voluntarily underwent all that his followers would be required to do after him—he trod the proper path. And the death of Jesus, when his blood was shed, had the closest possible relationship to the eucharist (e.g. Mark xiv. 22-5; 1 Cor. xi. 26). In the Johannine writings, this way of taking *v.* 7 may well coincide with the linking of the two words in GJ xix. 34 f. Though the tradition of exegesis did not, as far as we know, see a reference to the two sacraments in this emphatic statement until the fifth century,[1] this by no means proves that it was not at least part of what the writer meant.

Another passage in the Gospel may throw light on another pair among the three words linked in *v.* 7, GJ vii. 37 ff.; this time, water and Spirit. The passage is complex in the handling of the scriptural background to which it refers,[2] but the central image is that of Jesus as the new and true temple, the place where man is to meet God. The passage clearly looks ahead to his death and so to the incident at the crucifixion and on to the giving of the Spirit by the risen Christ (xx. 22). From him the life-giving water of baptism issues, fulfilling prophecies like Ezekiel xlvii. 1 ff. and Zech. xiv. 8 which foretold the pouring of torrents of water from beneath the temple in Jerusalem, to revivify the land, on the day of God's coming intervention. GJ iii. 5 had already associated water and Spirit with closer reference to baptism itself, seen as the way to new life.

It seems then that the writer makes first an anti-docetic point, in *v.* 6, then a sacramental point in *v.* 7. The two are closely related. Light is shed both on the link between the two and on the phrase **not water alone, but water and blood** by an account of the ideas of docetists, to be found in Ignatius' Letter to the Smyrneans, ch. vi f.: 'they have no faith in the blood of Christ.... They even absent themselves from the Eucharist and the public prayers, because they will not admit that the Eucharist is the self-same body of our Saviour Jesus Christ which suffered for our sins, and which the Father in his goodness afterwards raised up again.' The similarity with the teaching of those who are being attacked in 1J is obvious (cf. iv. 2; 2J 7).

There is one other possible bond between Spirit and the other

---

[1] For Patristic interpretations of this passage, see E. Hoskyns and F. N. Davey, *The Fourth Gospel*, London, 1940, pp. 534 f. It is not surprising that during the era of persecutions, **blood** should have been taken as signifying martyrdom and the incident, at the climax of Christ's passion, as giving to martyrdom the most solemn stamp of divine approval. There is no reason why this should have been the writer's intention.

[2] See R. E. Brown, *The Gospel According to John, I–XII*, New York, 1966, pp. 320 ff.; B. Lindars, *The Gospel of John*, London, 1972, pp. 297 ff.

two elements referred to in *v.* 7, and once more the Gospel provides the clue. At the meeting between the Baptist and Jesus at which in the other Gospels the baptism takes place, GJ speaks of the Spirit coming upon Jesus and 'dwelling'—it remained with him (the verb is *menō*, cf. pp. 81 f.). In xix. 30, Jesus' death is spoken of as the giving up of the spirit. It is a perfectly ordinary expression for dying; but perhaps it should be taken as the handing over (to the Father—or, looking ahead to xx. 22, the disciples?) of the Spirit—the Greek bears either sense. The death is then joined to the resurrection as the endowing of the disciples, and so of the Church, with the Spirit. So the Spirit is linked with the two moments in Jesus' career which the words **water** and **blood** evoke. All three together attest the reality of his death as the source of the life and power of the Church.

This understanding of the passage has most to be said in its favour; but it is not without rivals. The fact is that 'blood' is not elsewhere attested as a short-hand term for the eucharist, which we have taken to be the primary reference in *v.* 7. Where attention is drawn to one element alone to signify the whole rite, it is usually the bread or body which is singled out: cf. 1 Cor. x. 17; GJ vi; and, presumably, the miracles of feeding in the other Gospels, as well as passages like Mark viii. 14-21; Luke xxiv. 35; Acts ii. 42. But in GJ vi itself there is the idiosyncrasy of speaking in terms of 'flesh' rather than 'body', which is otherwise the usual eucharistic term; and at this early date there is no call to be surprised at a departure from what later became the dominant terminology. There was no list of approved technical terms!

It has also been suggested, in the light of this objection, that the reference in *v.* 7 is to baptism alone. Just as this is certainly the subject in GJ iii. 5 and perhaps in vii. 37 ff., so here (to adopt Nauck's statement of the matter), the Spirit is the gift received in baptism, water is the element used, and blood (i.e. Christ's death) is the source and basis for the rite. **The three are at one** in the sense that the meaning of all converges on the sacrament.[1]

As a result of his detailed study of this passage, Nauck makes another suggestion which has the merit of accounting for what seems on any showing a rather abrupt introduction of a reference to the eucharist—especially in a passage where plausibly baptismal

[1] See W. Nauck, *Die Tradition und der Charakter des ersten Johannesbriefes*, Tübingen, 1957, pp. 148 ff.

motifs are to the fore, such as the idea of witness and the treatment of sin (cf. v. 16 ff.), as well as the pervasive theme of Christians as God's offspring (e.g. ii. 29 ff.). A consideration of Patristic references and liturgical evidence, particularly of Syrian provenance, leads to the conclusion that the writer is alluding to the three significant elements in the initiation rite of the Johannine church: anointing, seen as the receiving of the Spirit, baptism and first admission to the eucharist. This certainly has the merit of linking the three very clearly. The association of anointing with initiation and with the gift of the Spirit finds confirmation in ii. 20: **You too have an anointing from the Holy One**. This last term, in Greek simply the adjective 'the Holy', may be short for 'the Holy Spirit', which, though not an expression used in 1J (he prefers simply 'the Spirit'), does occur in GJ xx. 22. The association finds confirmation also from the fact that both 'anointing' and 'Spirit' can be seen (together with **seed**, iii. 9) as alternative objective terms for God's endowment bestowed upon his chosen ones. Further, the statement in ii. 27 that the anointing by God is a means of teaching could be a reference to the instruction given in the community in connection with initiation into its membership.

Still, this order of the three elements (first Spirit, then water, then blood) is, in terms of later standard Christian practice, where baptism preceded both the rites associated with the gift of the Spirit and then communion, certainly unusual. But there is sufficient evidence that it existed precisely in circles with which the Johannine church is likely on other grounds to have affinities. The situation in the story told in Acts x (though not elsewhere in that book), where the gift of the Spirit precedes baptism, is perhaps the result merely of the absence of any firm dogmatism on the subject in the Lukan tradition or in the practice of the Lukan church; but both later Syrian Christian and contemporary Jewish practice speak more powerfully. In 1QS iii. 6-12 (Vermes, p. 75), purification of offenders by 'the spirit of holiness' precedes purification in water; and then the sinner is restored to the community and shares in table-fellowship: 'For it is through the spirit of true counsel concerning the ways of man that all his sins shall be expiated that he may contemplate the light of life. He shall be cleansed from all his sins by the spirit of holiness uniting him to his truth.... And when his flesh is sprinkled with purifying water and sanctified by cleansing water, it shall be made clean by

the humble submission of his soul to all the precepts of God.'
For what it is worth, the Testament of Levi (viii. 4 f.) refers to a
similar order of rites in connection with consecration to the priest-
hood: 'And the first (man) anointed me with holy oil.... The
second washed me with pure water, and fed me with bread and
wine' (Charles, II, p. 309).

The three unified witnesses[1] are in reality the vehicles of God's
own witness to himself, and if, in accordance with the Law, there
is common acceptance of two or three who testify in unison, then
all the more is God to be trusted. His testimony, expressed in **the
Spirit, the water and the blood,** concerned his Son (*v.* 9). The
verb (**has borne**) is in the perfect tense: it refers to the past act
of God in the life and death of Jesus. So the preaching and the
rites of the Church in the writer's own day are immediately
carried back once again to their historical basis—and the circle
is completed: from *v.* 6 to *v.* 7 and now in *v.* 9.

The believer in the Son (that is, in his historical and fleshly
reality) has in effect absorbed the testimony. He has accepted the
preaching and the power of the Spirit which it conveys (or possibly
he has been anointed in order to receive that power), he has
received baptism and he shares in the eucharist.

The writer is so convinced that God's witness to himself in the life
and death of Jesus is authentic that failure to believe the orthodox
faith is tantamount to accusing God of lying (cf. i. 10, p. 66).

According to *v.* 9, God's testimony consists in his having borne
testimony concerning his Son. Now, in *v.* 11, it consists in his
having given to us eternal life (cf. i. 2; ii. 25; GJ iii. 15; xx. 31).
In the former case, it is a matter of God's saving action in Jesus;
in the latter, of that which results from it. Each in its own way
shows the true nature of God. The two are intimately connected,
for the life which the believers receive is 'in' the Son, who was the
subject of the saving, earthly life which culminated in the real
death on the Cross. It is **in his Son,** that is, he is its basis and in
relationship with him alone can it be obtained. He defines the
sphere in which it is lived out and experienced. So absolutely is
this the case that (*v.* 12) to possess the Son is to possess life, and
to lack him is to belong to the sphere of death (cf. ii. 23, pp. 80 f.,
and GJ iii. 36).

---

[1] In this passage, the English words **witness** and **testimony** represent the
same Greek, *marturia* (and cognates).

# 9. ASSURANCE OF LIFE
## v. 13-21

(13) The purpose of my writing is that you may know that you have eternal life. It is written to those who believe in the name of the Son of God. (14) Our confidence in him is based on the fact that if we make requests in accordance with his will he hears us. (15) If we know that he hears our requests, then we also know that the requests we have made to him are granted. (16) If any of you sees his brother sinning, but not in such a way as to lead to death, he should pray, and God will grant him life—that is, in cases of non-deadly sin. There is such a thing as deadly sin. I do not say that a man should intercede about that. (17) All wrongdoing is sin, but there is sin which is not deadly. (18) We know that God's offspring does not sin; on the contrary, he holds on to God, and the Evil One does not touch him. (19) We know that we belong to God, while the entire world lies in the grip of the Evil One. (20) Yet we know that the Son of God has come, and has given us understanding so that we can know the True One. Indeed, we are in the True One—in his Son, Jesus Christ. This is the genuine God and he is eternal life. (21) Children, guard yourselves from idols.

In this section, with which the work closes (there is no formal farewell any more than there was an opening greeting), we meet once more familiar themes. But, just as we have found earlier, they appear in relation to one new matter: this time, intercession, in particular on behalf of members of the community who have fallen into sin. We have returned then to the issue with which the work began, but now the guidance is practical, whereas the earlier passage provided the doctrine (i. 8–ii. 2). Accordingly, it is less general, and the writer is forced to draw a distinction which was not needed before. Clearly, not all sins are of the same weight; there are those which bring the sinner into the sphere of death,[1]

[1] This way of taking the expression in *v.* 16 is prompted by the prevalence in 1J as a whole and in this particular context of the term 'life' for the sphere in

and those which are less serious. For the former, intercession
by the brothers is of no avail, but for the latter a favourable hearing
is assured.

Here, the intercessor, or advocate (we might easily have had
the noun), is one's fellow-Christian; in ii. 2 it was Christ himself.
What is the relationship between the one advocacy and the other?
And does the limited effectiveness promised to human intercession mean that Christ's intercession also is, in practice, in this
matter, limited in its effect—despite the wide, all-embracing
scope ascribed to it in the theological statement in ii. 2? We are
given no answer to these questions. All we can say is that our
present passage examines from the viewpoint of practical church
discipline a question raised earlier from the quite different angle
of doctrine.[1]

From another side, iii. 4-10 also seems to be inconsistent with
our present passage. There, the Christian does not and cannot sin,
so the question of seeking forgiveness does not arise. In fact, v. 18
says the same, and, for this passage at least, it becomes clear that
it states an ideal rather than the situation in the community.
Possibly that goes too for the earlier passage, but to put the matter
in terms of the ideal and the actual may fail to represent the
writer's position: see pp. 55 ff.

The distinction drawn between two classes of sin was familiar
in Judaism. In Lev. iv. 2 ff., Num. xv. 22-30 (cf. Heb. x. 26), we
find different treatment enjoined for sins committed inadvertently
and deliberate sins ('sins of the high hand'). Our present passage
does not make this the ground of distinction. Moreover, the
Pentateuchal passages have in mind largely the omission of ritual
duties, whereas the concern of 1J is presumably with moral
lapse.

The distinction between sin which leads to death and sin which
does not is found in the contemporary Testament of Issachar vii. 1;
the Testament of Gad iv. 6; and in Jubilees xxi. 22; xxvi. 34;

which adherents to God dwell or the possession which they have received.
'Death' would be the natural term for its antithesis. But the reference may be
more concrete: sins that **lead to death** may be those which carried that penalty
according to Jewish law. It is hard to say whether the practical note in this
passage is strong enough to make this sense more likely than the more metaphysical one. It is worth noting that neither in GJ nor in 1J is there any mention
of anything like the concept of Hell.

[1] For the idea of intercession for sin in the Old Testament, see W. Eichrodt,
*Theology of the Old Testament*, II, London, 1967, pp. 450 ff.

xxxiii. 13, 18. The last passage will serve as an example: 'And..,
Moses,..do according to these words, and not commit a sin unto
death; for the Lord our God is judge, who respects not persons
and accepts not gifts' (Charles, II, p. 64). And the Qumran community distinguished between light and deliberate sins: 'Every
man who enters the Council of Holiness and who deliberately or
through negligence transgresses one word of the Law of Moses,
on any point whatever, shall be expelled....But if he has acted
inadvertently, he shall be excluded from the pure Meal and the
Council.... For one sin of inadvertence (alone) he shall do penance
for two years. But as for him who has sinned deliberately, he shall
never return; only the man who has sinned inadvertently shall
be tried for two years that his way and counsel may be made
perfect according to the judgement of the Congregation' (1QS
viii f., Vermes, pp. 86 f.). Whether the basis of the distinction is the
same as that intended in 1J or not, clearly the two communities
are tackling the same problem. The guidance provided in the
Community Rule of the Dead Sea sect is more explicit and more
practical than that given to the Johannine church. On the face
of it, it also looks more severe.

If we try to envisage the situation which prompts our writer to
raise the matter and lay down his policy, then it may be that some,
perhaps the heretics, were inclined to eliminate some acts, considered sinful by the writer, from the category of sin altogether.
Our writer will not accept that: **all wrongdoing is sin** (*v.* 17),
even if distinctions can rightly be drawn between one sin and
another.

The Jewish writings to which we have referred are much closer
to the Johannine passage than other New Testament treatments of
the problem of post-baptismal sin. Heb. x. 26 knows the category
of deliberate sin and holds out no hope for those guilty of it; but
it is silent on the subject of a lesser category of sin which might
receive less severe treatment (cf. vi. 4 ff.; xii. 15 f.). A group of
Gospel sayings distinguish between forgivable and unforgivable
sin—the latter being defined as blasphemy against the Holy Spirit
(Mark iii. 29; cf. Matt. xii. 31 f.; Luke xii. 10); but it is not clear
that the reference is to sins committed by Christians, and the
indication is that it is not. It is probable that each evangelist had
his own idea of what was covered by this vague and enigmatic
expression, and we have no reason to suppose that the writer of

1J had any of them in mind. Other attempted solutions to the problem in the early Church are reflected in Hermas (*Similitudes*, vi. 2, see J. B. Lightfoot, *The Apostolic Fathers*, London, 1891, pp. 354 f.), where it is held that sin short of blasphemy may be repented of and forgiven; and in Matt. xviii. 21 f.; Luke xvii. 4 (which may refer only to private dealings); and Luke xv. 11 ff., where the picture is of God's gracious reception of sinners, though it is not clear whether erring members of the Church are at all in mind. The specific case of lapsed Christians is treated with great generosity in Matt. xviii. 12-14.

If we wish to be more precise and guess what our writer particularly holds to be sin unto death, then the context surely indicates that it is the holding of false faith. This is what 1J opposes from start to finish. And the sign of the holding of false faith is failure to love the brothers. Those who sin mortally are, in other words, those of whom the opposite of the dual statement in iii. 23 is true. They neither believe nor act rightly. Our writer has no other demands to make, no other concerns to express. The concern in i. 8 ff. may be with lesser sins, such as even the brothers commit.

There is much to be said for reading *v.* 13 not as the opening of a final paragraph, but as the ending—at an earlier stage in its history—of the whole work, the rest being a later postscript. In terms closely reminiscent of the ending of the main body of GJ (xx. 30 f., ch. xxi being similarly an appendix), this verse sums up the purpose of 1J in simple and succinct terms. There is one notable difference from GJ xx. 31. The Gospel is said to have been written 'that you may believe...and, believing, may have life in his name'. It is written to promote faith and the eternal life which is its fruit. 1J, on the other hand, has been written to promote not faith but knowledge—here in the sense of awareness—among those who already believe and already possess that fruit. It has been written, in other words, to reinforce the believers exposed to threats to their faith and inclined to waver in their recognition of the status that has been given to them. The views and the society of the heretics press upon them.

But the symmetry of theme between the first chapter of the Epistle and these final verses must stand as evidence that the work's final version was planned to include them, and it points to the importance of this theme to the writer. The question of right belief and of brotherly love carries with it, for the pastor of the church, the question of discipline. Whatever is true of the rest of the work, this final section looks as if it was composed for the work and did not exist as an independent piece in the devotional or homiletic repertory of the Johannine church. It is quite devoid of the aphoristic parallelism which dominates the earlier sections and lacks great Johannine words.

*V.* 13 begins, literally, 'I have written these things in order that you may know....' The aorist of the verb *graphō* ('write') has already occurred in ii. 14, 21, 26, but in none of these cases, except perhaps the last, is the pastness very important—the present tense would have done just as well (cf. ii. 12 f., p. 71). But here the past tense is deliberate and the addition of 'these things' shows that the writer is summing up the whole work. This is true whether he had a little more to say or originally meant to end at this point.

The Christians' confidence before God has been mentioned several times before—in relation to the return of Christ (ii. 28) and the day of Judgement (iv. 17), but also, as here, in present Christian life (iii. 21). In this earlier passage and in v. 14, this confidence is exercised in making requests. The true believer is assured of a hearing—that is, he is assured that his requests will be granted (GJ xvi. 23 f., where 'in my (= Christ's) name' is equivalent to **in accordance with his will** here). With God, to hear his children's prayers is to grant them. But the only subject of intercession mentioned is the erring brother and to that the writer speedily turns. It is in line with his singleness of mind and purpose. Everything is seen in the light of the shock given by the disruption of the community at the hands of the heretics. That disruption is enough to convince him that the End is at hand; love is strictly love for the Christian brothers; and now prayer is to be made for those who risk departure from the circle of light, and treatment is prescribed. But, by definition, brothers do not sin mortally.

The passage continues (*v.* 18), as we have seen, with a restatement of the strong meat of iii. 9: to be a Christian is to have immunity from the power of the Evil One and so from the sin of which he is the source. If a man does fall into serious sin, it is a proof that he is not a child of God—whatever the appearances may have been (cf. the form of argument in ii. 19). Then follows a formulation as pessimistic about the world as that in ii. 15 f., and even more absolute: **the entire world lies in the grip of the Evil One**.

It is then vital to hold to the faith and reality to which one has been admitted. This is no mere speculation but solid truth, and it has a content which the mind can grasp. It can be simply stated: **that the Son of God has come.** We dwell in him and in God whom he revealed. God is described by one of the Johannine church's central terms, *alēthinos*, 'true'. It is also one of its strongest terms: it signifies that which is real and genuine, as against that which is secondary and false (cf. p. 66, and for the expression here, cf. GJ xvii. 3). To be 'in' God is the same as to be 'in' his Son. Nowhere else in this writing are the two so completely identified.[1] We are reminded much more of the language of GJ (i. 1; x. 30; xx. 28) than of anything else here. And even in this verse, there is no doctrinal elaboration, merely the assertion. Usually, as we have seen, the christology of this work is less 'advanced' than that of GJ and it is hard to tell how far this is really an exception (cf. p. 14).

But with this qualification, we may say that 1J ends as it began—with an affirmation of the high status of Jesus and his mission. If it may not be quite true of this writer to say that 'he is what God is' (cf. GJ i. 1, NEB), yet he is 'God to us' and 'he gives what God gives', that is—eternal life (cf. *v.* 11). For this there is no substitute: **guard yourselves from idols**. These idols were not far too seek. The faith stated in *v.* 20 is exactly what the heretics deny, and their teaching is an appalling parody of the truth.

At Qumran too, the word *idol* was used: for the false and evil things of the heart (1QS ii. 11-17; iv. 5). And if that is the sense here, the writer knows whence they will be inspired—by the heretics who seek to lead his people astray from the one true God. They are 'antichrists' (ii. 18)—false deities. The devil they serve is linked with the false gods of the pagan world. In the face of such a crisis as they present, the tests of true faith must be clear and the boundary of truth plain.

[1] With the result that the suggestion has been made that we have here a gloss made on the strength of later orthodox formulation. There is no manuscript evidence to support this.

# THE SECOND EPISTLE OF JOHN

## TRUTH AND LOVE

(1) The Elder to a lady chosen by God and to her children, whom I love in truth—and not I alone but all who know the truth—(2) on account of the truth which dwells in us and will be with us for ever. (3) Grace, mercy and peace will be with us from God the Father and from Jesus Christ, the Son of the Father, in truth and love.

(4) I was delighted to find some of your children walking in the way of truth, just as the Father commanded us. (5) And now I ask you, my lady, not by way of a new command, but one we have had from the beginning: let us love one another. (6) Love means walking according to his commands. The command is, as you heard from the beginning, that you walk along the path it lays down. (7) For many deceivers have gone out into the world, people who do not acknowledge Jesus Christ as coming in the flesh. Such folk are the Deceiver and Antichrist. (8) Be careful not to lose what we worked for, but receive your reward in full. (9) Anyone who runs on ahead and does not dwell in the teaching of Christ does not possess God. He who does dwell in the teaching possesses both the Father and the Son. (10) If anyone comes to you and does not bring this teaching, do not receive him into your home and do not greet him. (11) To greet such a one is to share in his evil deeds.

(12) I have much to write to you, but do not wish to send it by pen and ink. Rather, I hope to come to you and talk face to face. This will make our joy complete. (13) The children of your chosen sister send their greetings.

From one point of view, the Second Epistle of John is a shadowy, faceless little work, and if it were necessary to declare redundant one item in the New Testament canon, it would be highly eligible. There is little in it of a doctrinal nature which does not occur in virtually identical terms in 1J, little of a circumstantial kind which is not paralleled (though the situation is not identical) in 3J.

Impressed by this and by the shortage of personal details, Bultmann (Commentary, p. 102) wonders whether the epistolary form is a fiction: the writer has decked a brief doctrinal manifesto, essentially of the same genre as 1J, in this guise by means of a top and a tail drafted in from 3J. (Others before him have expressed the same doubt about the genuineness as letters not only of 2J but also of 3J.) The audience, he suggests, is not a particular congregation, or he would have mentioned names as in 3J, but all those within his sphere of responsibility who stand in need of care or correction from him or his agents (cf. 3J 9 f.). The epistolary form then is no more genuine here than, many would hold, in the case of the Epistle to the Ephesians.

It could then be a derivative work, a minor weapon in the Johannine campaign; less weighty than 1J, less direct in impact than 3J, and having no notable characteristics of its own. It is symptomatic that in lists of references to Johannine themes, a mention of a verse in 2J commonly appears at the end, like a weak, dependent member of the Johannine household, included in the party out of politeness; only rarely do works from this writing merit independent attention. And in the reconstruction of the circumstances in which the various Johannine writings arose, which we hazarded in the Introduction, the Second Epistle hardly entered the discussion: it may be slipped in anywhere or nowhere —most naturally under the shadow of one of the other Epistles.

But now that we are examining it in its own right, let us see if there is not some way of rescuing it from this position of indignity. There is just one possibility, and we shall never know whether it corresponds to the truth. If this is a genuine letter, then it concludes with the expressed intention of the writer to visit his correspondents rather than writing to them at greater length. Whether he was able to satisfy his preference for the spoken to the written word, we cannot tell. But supposing that he was not, then perhaps he had after all to write more fully concerning the Christian truth by which he stood and the dire threats to which it was exposed: he had, he said, **much to write to** them (*v.* 12). It would be hard to find a more suitable lead into the First Epistle. If 2J may be regarded as a brief statement of the central message of 1J, which now overshadows it, the latter may equally be seen as an expanded version of the shorter work. In effect, it is the full statement of the position which 2J sketched out. This conjecture, giving to 2J a position of dignity in the affairs of the Johannine church, may go some way towards accounting for the survival of a short work whose independent importance seems otherwise to be minimal.

In form, if not in historical reality, 2J, like 3J but not 1J, is a letter. It observes the epistolary conventions of the Hellenistic world less well than 3J, but its divergence from ordinary models is accounted for by its religious message and is paralleled in the existing Christian literature of this genre, in particular the Epistles of Paul. The opening of a letter had three ingredients, the name of the writer, the name of the person addressed, and an expression of greeting (generally, the verb 'to greet', *chairein*). In the letters of Paul (e.g. 1 Cor. i. 1-3; Phil. i. 1 f.), all three were commonly elaborated by the addition of statements concerning the status of both writer and recipients and by greetings in language of theological significance. Like them, 2J, it appears, is more than a merely personal letter, but, again like them, that does not in the least mean that the letter-form is pure smoke-screen. As far as the last two ingredients are concerned, our writer does the same as Paul. He describes himself, however, simply as **the Elder**. On the meaning of that word, see pp. 4 f.

The identity of the letter's intended recipients is described less straightforwardly and has been from early times a matter of both confusion and speculation. There are two sources of possible difficulty, one initially a matter of the syntax, the other a matter of meaning. First, we must give a literal translation of the opening words: 'the Elder to the elect lady and to her children'. In the phrase 'elect lady' each of the two words (*eklektē kuria*) could be a proper name, so that besides the translation we have adopted, we could say either 'the lady Eklektē' or 'the elect Kuria'. The former of these possibilities, unlikely as it is, was adopted in the Latin translation, if not the original, of the Hypotyposes of the late second-century writer, Clement of Alexandria. The Epistle is said to be addressed 'to a Babylonian woman named Electa who signifies the catholic Church'. But *eklektos* is so common in early Christian literature as a description of believers (cf. Rom. viii. 33; xvi. 13; Col. iii. 12; 1 Peter i. 1; Rev. xvii. 14), that it is virtually certain to be used here as an adjective.

What then of *kuria*? Equivalent to Martha in Aramaic, it is a well-attested proper name. But a glance at *v.* 13 begins to turn us in another direction. Is the Johannine community, under the Elder, a multi-headed matriarchal society, and, what is more, so largely a female business? And does the body of 2J read like an item in a domestic correspondence, with particular attention given to feminine interests? Are we really in the presence of a Christian family whose junior members, so much under mother's wing, are becoming divided between those who live by 'the truth' and those who do not?

Or is **lady** rather a *façon de parler*? Is it not much more likely to signify, like the sister in *v.* 13, a Christian congregation? Perhaps it is a specific group, or, in view of the absence of the definite article, any one of a number of Johannine churches where the same characteristics are to be found. There is no exact parallel to such an expression elsewhere in the New Testament, but there are close approximations. In 2 Cor. xi. 2, Paul speaks of the Corinthian congregation as the betrothed of Christ, and the image reappears, applied to the whole Church, in Eph. v. 22 ff. and, similarly, to the New Jerusalem, in Rev. xxi. 2. Behind it lies the common Old Testament description of Israel or Jerusalem as a young woman, Yahweh's bride, bound to him in covenant (Ex. xxxiv. 15; Is. liv. 5; Hos. i–iii; Zeph. iii. 14 ff.; Zech. ix. 9). It appears in the Johannine writings in GJ iv. 16-26, where the woman probably symbolizes the Samaritan people as a whole, and perhaps in ii. 1-11 and xix. 25-27, with the mother of Jesus standing for expectant Israel. Here, the idea, inherent in the image, of the bond between God and his people, is expressed in the word **chosen**, *eklektē* (cf. in LXX, Ps. civ. 6; Is. xlii. 1). It is paralleled in 1 Peter v. 13, where the cognate adjective of the same meaning, *suneklektē*, is used, probably intending the noun 'church' to be understood (some manuscripts include it).

The word **truth** dominates the opening of the Epistle, *vv.* 1-3, and indeed it is in effect the main concern of the whole work, though the term itself does not occur after *v.* 4. What degree of profundity of sense does it bear? The first occurrence, **in truth** (*v.* 1), may mean no more than 'truly', 'really'; though it means more in 3J 3 and perhaps in 1J iii. 18. But everything that we know of the general Johannine use of the word, and indeed the manner of its use in the next few lines, leads us to see it carrying its fullest meaning.

R. Bergmeier ('Zum Verfasserproblem des II und III Johannes-

briefes', *ZNW*, 57, 1966, pp. 93 ff.) maintains that as in the
Pastoral Epistles the dominant concern here, by contrast with GJ,
is not with a speculative picture of reality in which 'truth' and
'falsehood' are the two poles of a dualistic scheme, but with
orthodoxy of teaching. 'The truth' signifies the Christian faith
as the writer holds it. It is equivalent to **the teaching** of *v.* 9.

But this would mean driving a wedge between 1J and 2J in this
matter, for there, alongside the strong concern for orthodoxy, the
dualistic framework is undeniable; and we have no reason to
suppose that any great gap separates the one from the other in
time or circumstance. Moreover, the use of **truth** in these verses,
with a whole galaxy of doctrinally weighty Johannine terms, **know,
dwell, love** and **walk**, speaks against Bergmeier's view; and the
use of **dwell** with **the teaching** in *v.* 9 does not compel us to
'lighten' the sense of **truth** to make it conform to the more concrete word. As in 1J, **truth** is the sphere in which God's genuine
saving doctrine, expressed in Christ, is realized, assured and
enjoyed (cf. p. 66). Even **I love in truth** may see this sphere as
the scene of the love which the Elder can only bestow because he
has received it from God (cf. 1J iv. 19; 2J 5 f.).

That the situation envisaged in this work is much the same as
that in 1J is apparent from the start. The very stress on truth, and
the almost immediate parenthesis (**and not I alone but all who
know the truth**), betray a certain assertiveness: there are those,
only too plainly, who do not know the truth, and from them the
writer is keen to dissociate himself (cf. *vv.* 10 f.). In the congregation addressed, it may be that they predominate: such is the
impression given by *v.* 4. So the writer's love (*v.* 1) is conditional
on community in the truth between him (and his associates) and
those to whom he writes—not as a matter of will or emotion on his
part so much as by the constraint of divine realities: love binds
those who have been brought by God to dwell in the circle of
light as his offspring (cf. p. 62).

The greeting in *v.* 3 repeats the **with us** of *v.* 2, but moves away
from the Johannine **truth** to three terms of wider, indeed in
Christian writings conventional, currency: **grace, mercy and
peace**. All three occur in the greetings of other epistles, whether
exactly as here (as in 1 Tim. i. 2 and 2 Tim. i. 2) or in various
combinations (e.g. Jude 2; 1 Cor. i. 3; Phil. i. 2; Col. i. 2), 'grace
and peace' being particularly characteristic of Paul. All three

derive from Old Testament usage, where they signify various aspects of God's gracious and saving relationship with his people; and there too they commonly occur in pairs. Quite often 'truth' appears in combination with one of the other words (cf. in LXX, 'mercy and truth' in Josh. ii. 14; Ps. xxiv. 10; xxxix. 11; lxxxiv. 10; 'truth and peace' in Jer. xiv. 13; Zech. viii. 19). GJ itself has 'grace and truth' in i. 14, 17. Of the trio, **grace** (four times in GJ, once each in 2J and 3J) and **mercy** (here only) are not great Johannine words; though **peace** appears in GJ xiv. 27; xvi. 33; and xx. 19, 21, 26. Except in the case of the last word, it may be doubted whether the sense is as strong theologically as, for example, in the case of 'grace' in Pauline usage, and the three words here may not be much more than a formula. Nevertheless, **peace** seems to carry in Johannine usage its Old Testament weight: it denotes a richness and wholesomeness of relationship between man and man or man and God generally lacking in the modern use of the word. It is of course the common Jewish salutation (cf. 3J 15).

It is hard to see that the final phrase in *v.* 3, **in truth and love**, adds substantially to the sense. It is a piling on of the writer's key words.

Hellenistic letter-writers (like modern ones) commonly followed up the greeting with a reference to something which had pleased them or moved them to gratitude (to the friend or to the gods) in the words or activities of their correspondents. Paul usually expresses thanks to God at this point for some benefit in connection with the Christians to whom he writes (e.g. 1 Cor. i. 4; Phil. i. 3), and he elaborates considerably on the conventional pattern. Our present writer (cf. 3J 4) sticks closer to it. In simple terms, he expresses his pleasure that some members of the congregation have remained faithful to the path of truth.

At this point, as we move from the phrase **walking in the way of truth** to **as the Father commanded us**, there is an important but not untypical shift in his thought. *V.* 5 tells, in the common Johannine manner, what the command is: **let us love each other** (cf. GJ xiii. 34; 1J iii. 11), and, as in 1J ii. 7 (cf. p. 67), its deep roots in the story of the Christian community are affirmed. But in *v.* 4 the command is stated in terms of **walking in the way of truth**, and **truth**, we have said in relation to *vv.* 1–3, is the sphere of genuine and reliable divine reality. To stay in that sphere is hardly a matter of command, it is a providence of God. And it concerns status not morals. But **walk** is an ethical as well as a 'status' term, and though there is in Johannine thought a sense of finality about the assignment of a man to the sphere of light or of darkness, of truth or of falsehood, obedience to the command to love is repeatedly invoked as both its expression and its test (cf. p. 97). The shift in *v.* 4 from the one dimension to the other is both smooth and characteristic.

*V.* 6 has one of our writer's familiar reversals of previous formulations. He loves to combine his favourite words in all possible directions. So in 1J iii. 6, for example, 'the man who dwells in him does not sin'; then: 'everyone who sins...has not known him' (that is, virtually, does not dwell in him); and in iv. 12: 'if we love each other (i.e. do not sin), God dwells in us'. In 1J iii. 9, 'the offspring of God does not sin'; then, in iv. 7: 'everyone who loves (i.e. does not sin) is born of God'. And here: while in *v.* 5 we learnt that the command was that we should love each other, now we hear, first, that **love means walking according to his commands**, then, by a further shake of the kaleidoscope, that **the command is** (literally) 'that you walk in it' (i.e. the command) —taken by itself, and without the attempt at improving disguise which we have made in our translation, a pretty barren piece of moralizing!

At this point (*v.* 7), we turn back to matters of faith, and to the dangerous heresy which has arisen to afflict the congregation. To counter it, the writer brings both doctrine and practical action. The transition is less abrupt than it seems. It is a failure to adhere to the strict path of love, and so of unity, which has led some into error: the word rendered **deceivers** (*planoi*) is cognate with the verb 'to go astray', i.e. instead of walking in the true path (*v.* 6). Their moral and doctrinal failures are intimately related; and now the heretics have **gone out** from the church, they are a seductive threat to those who remain. The note of warning, anxiously sounded, is strong. For the heresy, see pp. 14 f. (and cf. 1J ii. 18-22). The description of it here is virtually identical with 1J iv. 2, except that the verb ('come') is in the present rather than perfect participle. It is most improbable that this can be taken to mean that the reference is to Christ's future coming; **in the flesh** would be unlikely, though not impossible, for that purpose. For what it is worth, GJ vi. 14 and xi. 27 show comparable usage: whether it is right to see in this present participle, especially in our present verse (but even in the Gospel references), 'a timeless description of Jesus, as God's emissary into the world' (Bultmann, Commentary, p. 107) is open to doubt: our writer is usually keen in this regard to emphasize the full human reality of the Messiah Jesus of the earthly life. **Such folk** is, literally, 'this'. As in 1J ii. 18, the Antichrist is identified absolutely with the heretical group, singular with plural.

*V.* 8 introduces language without close Johannine parallel, except GJ vi. 27 ff., where, as here no doubt, the reward is seen as eternal life. But cf. also Gal. iv. 11; Mark ix. 41; and, for the final expression, Ruth ii. 12.

A final statement of the heresy follows in *v.* 9, and its effect for those who hold it is stated in terms very close to those of 1J ii. 23 (cf. *v.* 12). The heresy itself is described in two ways. First, as 'running on ahead' (*proagō*)—the image of keeping to a path once more (*vv.* 6 f.). Second, as 'not dwelling in the teaching of Christ'. In 1J ii. 23, it is denying or acknowledging the Son which determines 'possession' of God. Are these terms equivalent? The expression in 1J is almost certainly doctrinal: it is a matter of acknowledging, or refusing to acknowledge, that the Son of God is none other than the human Jesus. **The teaching of Christ** is ambiguous. It may mean the doctrine concerning him, and so be equivalent in sense to the passage in 1J; but it may refer to Jesus' teaching, specifically no doubt, the command to love (cf. for the Johannine use of **teaching** (*didachē*), GJ vii. 16 f., where the sense is wider). As we have seen, failure to hold to doctrinal or moral orthodoxy is equally pernicious in the eyes of our writer, equally dire in its effects.

Theoretical condemnation is not enough; there must also be practical measures. This passage (*vv.* 10 f.) has, on any showing, an ugly look, but if we reflect upon the close-knit character of the early Church and the ready extension of hospitality in which it found expression, then it is even more drastic and unfortunate. Lacking any machinery of regular conferences or councils, the early Church seems to have relied for such internal cohesion as it possessed largely upon frequent visits between congregations. The welcoming of such visitors (but with a wary eye for impostors, cf. Didache xi–xii, *ECW*, pp. 232–4) ranked high in the catalogue of virtuous acts (Rom. xii. 13; 1 Tim. v. 10; Heb. xiii. 2; 1 Peter

iv. 9; cf. Matt. x. 11-14). How serious then was the decision to refuse such hospitality and to deny the greeting that symbolized friendship. Our writer was not the only Christian leader to move in this direction about this time: cf. Jude 23; Ignatius, Eph. vii. 1; viii. 1; Smyr. iv. 1; v. 1; vii. 2; in *ECW*. He saw continued fellowship of any kind as in effect sharing in the heretics' **evil deeds**. What those deeds were he does not specify: whether their spreading of their doctrine, their failures in love or other misdeeds.

These verses have no parallel in 1J; but in 3J we find a situation where the boot is on the other foot, so much so that one could even imagine Diotrephes, the blackguard of 3J, as the author of 2J: his policy is that which is here enjoined. In 3J the agents of the Elder are themselves suffering the refusal of hospitality (3J 10). It is impossible to say whether the unlikely possibility mentioned above has in it any shred of truth, equally impossible to say whether 3J describes the same set of relationships as 2J at a different stage in their development or whether different congregations are involved in the two cases.

The letter closes. The first part of the conclusion is identical in sense with 3J 13 f., though not sufficiently so in words to be necessarily a copy (as has been suggested, cf. p. 140, and contrast Col. iv. 7 f. = Eph. vi. 21 f.). **Pen and ink** is, literally, 'paper and ink'; NEB has 'in black and white'. And **face to face** is, literally, 'mouth to mouth' (cf. Num. xii. 8). The final clause of *v.* 12 is virtually the same as 1J i. 4. In both cases **our** is likely to be an official or editorial plural. *V.* 13 harks back to the idiom of *v.* 1: the Elder ends by associating with himself the congregation to which he belongs. Unlike 3J, this is essentially a letter from one church to another rather than a personal communication; though in the intimate and close-knit mode of life in the early Church, the distinction is far from rigid (cf. Philemon). The concluding greeting is conventional and, unlike Paul's (and others', cf. Rev. xxii. 21) use of 'grace be with you' in such contexts (e.g. Phil. iv. 23), there is no specifically Christian feature. For that reason perhaps, some manuscripts insert the phrase here. The **much** (*polla*) which begins *v.* 12, as also 3J 13, is reminiscent of GJ xx. 30, where the Gospel's probable original conclusion also opens with this word: a minor symptom of an early Christian group which was much given to sticking to its favourite words and expressions?

# THE THIRD EPISTLE OF JOHN

## TROUBLES IN THE CHURCH

(1) The Elder to dear Gaius, whom I love in truth. (2) My dear, I pray that all may go well with you and that you may be in good health, as it goes well, I know, with your soul. (3) I was delighted when brothers came and testified to your faithfulness to the truth. You are indeed walking in the truth. (4) I have no greater joy than to hear that my children walk in the path of truth. (5) Dear friend, you are loyal indeed in doing so much for the brothers, even though they are strangers to you. (6) They have testified to your love in the presence of the congregation. Please do good to them by sending them forward on their journey in a manner worthy of God. (7) It was for the sake of the Name that they went out; and they accepted nothing from pagans. (8) So we have an obligation to support such men, in order to be fellow-workers with them in the cause of the truth.

(9) I wrote a letter to the congregation. But that power-hungry man of theirs, Diotrephes, refused to receive us. (10) So if I come, I shall bring up the things he does: he speaks evil of us and makes false accusations against us- And not satisfied with that, he refuses to receive the brothers, hinders those who want to do so and expels them from the church.

(11) Dear friend, imitate not the evil but the good. He who does good is born of God; he who does evil has never seen God. (12) Demetrius gets a good testimonial from everybody, and from the truth itself. We ourselves endorse this testimony, and you know that our testimony is true.

(13) I had a great deal to write to you, but I prefer not to communicate by pen and ink. (14) Rather, I hope to see you soon, and we shall talk face to face. (15) Peace be with you. Our friends greet you. Greet our friends, every one.

The circumstances surrounding the writing of the Third Epistle received considerable attention in our Introduction (pp. 1 ff.). With the numerous references to individuals and groups, those circumstances are well defined, compared to the blur which, in this respect, surrounds the other two Epistles. We used 3J therefore as the foundation of our speculative attempt to give an account of the events reflected in the Johannine corpus as a whole and particularly in the Epistles. More clearly than the Gospel, they arise from specific circumstances in the Johannine congregations—a crisis of unity and faith. As we saw, not all scholars agree that the three Epistles arise from essentially the same situation, even if at different stages in its development; but it cannot be denied that in reflecting the presence of schism in the church they are at one. The Third Epistle has the value of presenting that picture in concrete terms.

Its demerit is to be light on doctrine. By comparison with 1J and 2J, it tells us nothing of the teaching for which the writer so firmly stands—except that it is 'the truth'. This has led to the view (p. 9) that the silence is deliberate: on this matter the writer felt vulnerable and it was safer to stick to generalities. He was conscious of being out of step with the main body of the Church's teaching—of which Diotrephes was (on this view) the champion. Such a drastic reinterpretation not only removes 3J from its close family connections with the other two Epistles (and those connections need to be convincingly accounted for); it also insists unreasonably on the Johannine writer putting pen to paper always and only in order to cover it with combinations of his doctrinal key words. Is he not to be permitted even a brief communication of a more personal kind, just once in a Johannine (canonical) epistolary career?

Moreover, doctrinal elements are not as lacking in 3J as may at first sight appear. 'Truth' occurs six times, once more than in 2J, and 'true' once (never in 2J). And though it is never elaborated or expounded in 3J, our experience of both 1J and 2J does not impel us to dismiss the word as a mere cliché—or as the rhetoric of a man who wants to make the best of a weak case.

The three Epistles treat a situation in many ways similar at different levels. It is true that there is apparent a deterioration from 1J to 2J, and from 2J to 3J—deterioration in the sense that the assertiveness of the schismatics seems to grow (it has come to a head in the activities of Diotrephes), and that the division between the two sides hardens into an increasing denial of friendship on both sides (2J 10 f.; 3J 10). Whether the conflict is confined to one dependent church or not, it is impossible to be sure. But the dispute over 'the truth' is the heart of the matter. In 1J the doctrinal remedies are prescribed and applied; in 2J action is added. In 3J we have arrived at the level of personalities.

The opening greeting is of the simplest kind, according to the conventions of the time, and its only deviation from the norm is the phrase **I love in truth**, instead of 'greeting' (*chairein*). Like many close-knit societies, the Johannine church has its catch-phrases: cf. 2J 1. And though **in truth** can well mean no more than 'truly' (cf. p. 142), the use of this resonant Johannine word in this phrase, used in deviation from the norm, may indicate that it bears its deeper sense. Common participation in 'the truth' binds Johannine Christians to each other and is the ground of their love.

On the station of **the Elder**, cf. pp. 4 f. That of Gaius is not clear, but presumably he is a leader of those in the divided congregation who remain loyal to 'orthodoxy' (cf. *v.* 15); and he may have been one of the Elder's converts—he describes him as one of his **children** (*tekna*) in *v.* 4, cf. 1 Cor. iv. 14; Phil. ii. 22 (though there is no strong reason to see this implication necessarily in the frequent use of the related word *teknia* in 1J (ii. 1 etc.)). The name is Roman in origin and very common (cf. in the NT itself, Rom. xvi. 23; 1 Cor. i. 14; Acts xix. 29; xx. 4). Our study of the theological affinities of 1J led to the conclusion that Jewish influences were dominant in the formation of Johannine thought. These congregations, like so many in the early Church, were probably mixed in their composition.

**Dear friend** (*v.* 2; cf. *vv.* 5, 11), literally, 'beloved one', *agapēte*: this address occurs in the plural six times in 1J (never in 2J). Like 'truth', it is, in Johannine writing, never likely to be used casually. Love, *agapē*, is the God-given bond uniting the Christian brothers and constituting their deepest obligation to each other.

For the sentiments of *vv.* 2 f., cf. p. 144. The conventional expression of pleasure at the correspondent's physical health gives place to concern with his total welfare, as the succeeding verses proceed to show. **Soul**, as in later religious usage, signifies *in effect* 'the spiritual side', but we should be wrong to press any dualistic or negative implications of such a rendering. Though the Johannine Epistles have no favourable attitude to 'the world' (e.g. 1J ii. 15 f.), they are too Jewish to accept a formal and explicit division of man into 'body' and 'soul', with depreciation of the former. As in OT usage, the Johannine writings mean by *psuchē* (translated **soul**) 'life', cf. 1J iii. 16; GJ x. 11. That life is seen here in its relationship with God.

There is an abundance of coming and going between the Johannine congregations: for this feature of early Church life and its importance, cf. p. 146; and for the expression of Gaius' orthodoxy, cf. 2J 4; 1J ii. 6. For the writer's **joy** inspired by his flock's hold on true doctrine, cf. 1J i. 4.

Orthodoxy is tested in action (*v.* 5). In particular, those who share right belief receive and care for one another, quite beyond the limits of personal acquaintance. Gaius has risen admirably to the occasion, as members of the Elder's church have reported (*v.* 6). (**Congregation,** or 'church', *ekklēsia*, only here and *vv.* 9 f. in Johannine writings, apart from Revelation.) We have here a specific practical example of the duty of loving the brothers by which 1J (especially iv. 16 ff.) sets such great store in terms of theoretical exposition. It raises the question how far, in writing the exposition, the writer had this particular expression of brotherly love in mind. It was one of crucial importance to the Johannine churches—in effect, the maintenance of both fellowship and communication between them.

It comes as no surprise, given the intensely inward-looking quality of the Johannine consciousness (cf. p. 62), that those who maintain that communication by their travels choose to rely wholly on Christian resources. The Johannine world is resolutely self-contained (the tone is more exclusive than, e.g., Matt. x. 9 ff.; Mark ix. 40)—in deliberate separation from 'the world' at large. GJ xvii gives the theological rationale. These agents are thereby distinguished from the common run of contemporary travelling purveyors of philosophies and cults. Travelling emissaries who stick to this policy of shunning pagan help have a claim on their fellows: but heresy cancels the bond (*v.* 8; cf. 2J 10 f.). **Fellow-workers** (*sunergoi*) is otherwise in the NT a Pauline word (e.g. Rom. xvi. 3; Phil. ii. 25; Col. iv. 11). For the description of the Christian cause simply as *the Name* (i.e. of Christ or Jesus, *v.* 7), cf. Acts iv. 17; v. 41; 1 Peter iv. 14-16; also GJ xv. 21.

The opposition centres on Diotrephes. He is described as

*philoprōteuōn*, literally, 'loving to be in the first place' (**power-hungry** seeks to convey the distinctly pejorative flavour). His supporters would have referred to their leader more respectfully, perhaps given him one of the titles, such as 'bishop' or 'elder' then used for church leaders. From a dispassionate standpoint, he is almost certainly to be seen as one of a number of examples known to us of the emergence about this time of individuals to a position of leadership in a congregation. Here that emergence takes place in an atmosphere of strife. It is seen as a bid for independence, withdrawing a congregation from its loyalties; and worse, it is probably associated with doctrinal deviation. In the Pastoral Epistles (especially 1 Timothy), we see such an office arising in an atmosphere of comparative calm; but in the Letters of Ignatius (*ECW*, pp. 63 ff.), where one who is in some ways a Diotrephes writes on his own account, there are so many signs that the position needed asserting that we may guess all was not plain sailing, even if the conflict was on different grounds. By contrast with the situation in 2J 10 f., Diotrephes is strong enough to take the initiative in breaking off relations with the Elder (he rejected an earlier letter[1] from him) and his party (**the brothers**, *v*. 10). This he has done thoroughly.

The precise nature of Diotrephes' rebuttal of the Elder and his friends is unclear. The same verb (**receive**, *epidechomai*) is used in *v*. 9 and *v*. 10*b*; but in the first case, it seems to refer to the letter and so, presumably, to mean 'accept the message of', whereas in the second it refers to a physical refusal to see the Elder's emissaries, a refusal he may soon test for himself (cf. *v*. 14). The common ground is of course the teaching which the letter contained and which the messengers stood for and conveyed. **Us** in *v*. 9 (cf. *v*. 12) is either an editorial plural or more probably reflects the close identification between the Elder and his associates.

It is not possible to say what the expulsion from the congregation (*v*. 10) amounts to; in effect, we may presume, a separate gathering, centred on Gaius, of those whom the Elder can call his friends (*v*. 15). But it looks as if there remains at least enough contact between the two groups for the Elder to plan a confrontation (**I shall bring to mind**).

---

[1] There is no good reason to identify this with 1J or 2J, especially if, as Bultmann suggests (Commentary, p. 99), it dealt with the duty of hospitality, as *vv*. 3-8 indicate.

**Evil** in *v.* 11 no doubt refers particularly to the bitter schism-making and violation of brotherly love which is the main theme of this letter; and **good**, also precise, refers to their opposites. To 'do good' is, in Johannine terms, to love. So 1J iv. 7 has a virtual equivalent of *v.* 11: 'everyone who loves is born of God' (here, literally, 'is from God'), cf. also iii. 10*b*. Similarly, the last clause of *v.* 11 reproduces 1J iii. 6 (cf. p. 94). This antithesis is the only example in this Epistle of the form which is so pervasive in 1J. If behind that work there lay a collection of such aphorisms, then perhaps this belonged to it.

Demetrius (*v.* 12) enters unannounced. Most likely he is the bearer of the letter and this message is his accreditation. His own speech will bear out the approval given to him by the Elder and his friends (**everybody**); his beliefs are sound. (For this Greek name, cf. Acts xix. 24.)

The farewell is not very different from that in 2J (cf. p. 147). **Peace be with you** is the Jewish greeting, cf. Eph. vi. 23; 1 Peter v. 14. It was also Johannine—the greeting of the risen Jesus to his friends, GJ xx. 19, 21, 26.

# INDEX OF REFERENCES

## OLD TESTAMENT AND APOCRYPHA

# INDEX OF REFERENCES

## NEW TESTAMENT

# INDEX OF REFERENCES

# INDEX OF REFERENCES

# INDEX OF REFERENCES

# INDEX OF REFERENCES

# INDEX OF NAMES

# INDEX OF SUBJECTS

74 75 76 77 78 10 9 8 7 6 5 4 3 2 1